D1624331

When Are You Entitled to New Underwear and Other Major Financial Decisions

◆

Making Your

Money Dreams

Come True

◆

Eileen Michaels

Scribner

SCRIBNER
1230 Avenue of the Americas
New York, NY 10020

SCRIBNER and design are trademarks of Simon & Schuster Inc.

Designed by Brooke Zimmer
Set in Adobe Garamond
Manufactured in the United States of America

1 3 5 7 9 10 8 6 4 2

Library of Congress Cataloging-in-Publication Data
Michaels, Eileen.
When are you entitled to new underwear and other major financial
decisions : making your money dreams come true / Eileen Michaels.
p.   cm.
1. Women—Finance, Personal. I. Title.
HG179.M454   1997
332.024'042—dc20   96-43277
CIP

ISBN 0-684-81534-6

for my Bubbie Chasha

CONTENTS

IV. Security

V. Risk

VI. Choices

THANK YOU

To everyone in my family, a lot of this book is about you and the lessons I have taken from life with you. To my brother, Steve, who shared my childhood experiences and believed in my grown-up dreams . . . thanks for all the encouragement. Most important, to the original storytellers, my parents Millie and Sol Feinstein, and to the future storytellers, my children and grandchildren Andrew, Jonathan, Inger, Tyler, and Tiana. It is my honor and privilege to share you all with the people who did not know you before. You are the spirit and energy that keeps family alive and stories worth telling, and I love you very much.

To my agent, Harriet Wasserman. Thank you and thank you again!

To the incomparable Joyce Engelson, who taught me a thing or two about writing and about life.

To Susan Moldow, publisher, and Leigh Haber, my editor, at Scribner, who read the first unedited, unpolished, untitled version and understood what I was trying to communicate and bought the book!

To Neil Baim, Ira Blumberg, Oscar Hijuelos, Bruce Schaeffer, and Marjorie's sister, for your invaluable advice and assistance.

To my friends Lisa Callan, Curtis Cole, Dottie Galliano, Stuart Gelles, Marci Goldstein, Maggie Inge, Stanley Kirshenbaum, Phyllis Trinin, and Riki Wagman.

To my honored clients and business associates, with love and appreciation for all of your kind ways.

A very special thank-you to my associates at Legg Mason, and to my assistant, Michelle Lake.

I am a very lucky woman. Over the years I have been blessed with extraordinary people who have touched my life and taught me and supported me. The longer I live, the more I understand that nothing is ever done alone.

When Are You Entitled
to New Underwear
and
Other Major
Financial Decisions

INTRODUCTION

Before plastic there was cash, before cash there was coin, and before coin there was wampum. Always there was confusion and stress about money.

Money pays for the rent, the food, the baby clothes, education, and retirement. So, who wouldn't have powerful feelings about something that important in their lives?

Over the years we have become sophisticated, educated, and sensitive to financial matters. We know how little the dollar will buy, how far it will stretch, and how very important it is to save!

We are always questioning what is important to us and what really matters. Now, in order to be able to change our relationship to money and create the best for ourselves with what is available, we need to understand the critical role we play in how our financial lives turn out—and that *we do have choice all the time.*

What would you say if I told you that you could get a return of 14 or even 20 percent on your money—without any risk? Even better, you could improve your credit and decrease the stress you are feeling. The only thing you would need to do is change the way you think and arrange your finances. That's right!

You would probably be willing to scrimp and save to get money to invest so that you could get that very high return I'm talking about. You'd be really excited about making that much of a return on your money. Sounds good so far!

Now give me your credit cards for just one year. Every month we'll send the maximum payment you possibly can to the credit card company. New concept, maximum payment? Finance charges are eating away your ability to save real money, and I can tell you that each year you are paying a credit card company much more then you are earning on your money market or savings account. You earn 3 percent and you're paying 20 to the credit card company. It's costing you 17 percent to feel good. What, you're no longer interested? You thought I was telling you about a risk-free, guaranteed return, and now I'm only telling you to use those money market funds or the money in that savings account and pay off your Visa bill. Hey, but wait a minute, that *is* a risk-free, guaranteed return. After one year you will have saved all the interest charges on all the dollars you paid off. A tidy sum! So if the results are the same, how come you're not so excited? Paying off credit cards is not saving? Not a sexy enough idea? You don't want to give up your *extra* money and control of the plastic? Are you programmed to think that way? Maybe you need to rewire your circuit? Maybe you should rethink your relationship with money and how that translates to your entire life.

Somehow, money is still a very taboo subject. Most people would rather tell you about how they've behaved in bed with their partner than what balance they carry on their credit cards. If the 1980s produced conspicuous consumption and financial abuse, then the 1990s seem to be about self-doubt and guilt. Women especially find that they are having a hard time trying to figure out what they truly deserve: how to be smart, responsible, and create the security they crave in their financial lives.

My intention in writing this book is to bring openness to the discussion of money, especially for women. Remember, I'm talking about *money* here, not just investing. There are many good books and columns on investing, and you'll find a list of the books I recommend in the back of this book, but *first the subject to be clear about is money.* Understanding your relationship with money is much bigger than the dos and don'ts of investing. If we can open up, and accept without self-criticism, wherever we are in our present financial life, and see the possibility of change, we can create new ways of living to achieve our goals, and then take the action required to reach our financial desires—whatever they are.

Because few of us were taught about money in a direct and clear way, and as a result we're operating with confused and often incomplete information, it's no surprise that when we reach inside ourselves to find the financial knowledge we think we should have, it's not there. But there is no reason to feel wrong or stupid or full of self-doubt about this. After all, you were never taught about money in the first place. Knowing this will help you begin to feel free to change your relationship to money. And that's the process I hope to help you begin.

In order for us to achieve the success we are looking for in our money lives, we need to reintroduce the human element, which is so often missing, back into the money conversation: the *people dimension* of money, the real intimacy of what money means to you and the decisions you make about it every day.

Money has powerful psychological overtones. Our very survival is based on the use of money. It is—deeply—part of life itself. If I could get across only one philosophical point here, it would be that money is not a tiny compartment or section of life; it is your intimate partner. Whatever your politics, whatever your financial resources, you are deeply and forever in relationship with money.

If money has such an important and powerful position in our lives, then we have the right to understand how we function when we deal with it. If we don't understand the roles we play when it comes to decisions about money, then it stands to reason that we often don't feel satisfied with the outcome. We read magazine articles, take courses, talk to other people, and yet it seems that nothing much changes. So we are left feeling frustrated and dissatisfied with ourselves. What we're overlooking is the need to address our individual dreams and fantasies, our private unspoken thoughts, our internal whispers about what we should and should not do, when we should or should not have things, what we feel we are entitled to have in our lives. *The human dimension!*

In spite of the progress we've made I am still surprised by how often we women are embarrassed by what we do not know. As a result, we are often hard on ourselves. You can't be stupid if you were never taught in the first place. We also forget that we carry with us personal histories and experiences that often dictate today's choices. If we allow ourselves to take an inventory of what we are holding on to as truth about "the way things should be," and where we decided that, we can begin to move on. All the facts in the world about investing, the demon of credit card debt, or how much money it will take to retire may not produce an iota of difference if we don't become active participants in the process of our money lives, understanding what matters to us. *We are human beings with unique and valuable differences.*

Men and women both deal with issues about money. Their money issues may be different, but they are equally powerful. Men often wonder if they will do as well as their fathers did, or if they will cause family problems by being more successful than their fathers. Will there be jealousy or anger? Sometimes they are uncomfortable doing "better." Sometimes they feel tremendous pressure to be the "family hope," and sometimes they follow what others have done before them because "it's probably the right thing to do." But most men have some resource of information that they can turn to for reassurance. They have places they feel they can go to ask questions: they have been networking with each other for years. Men ask questions and expect to get them answered. Although understanding money may make them even more nervous or uncomfortable, they plunge forward (that is what's expected of them, isn't it?), getting on with their fact gathering and knowing whom to turn to for results. They remain high in hopes that somehow they will live up to whatever promises were made to the world when they were born. Unlike women, who often apologize for asking "stupid questions," most guys out there think that asking questions is a birthright and there are no stupid questions. I agree with them! As a matter of fact, the stupider that you feel a question is, the more you should ask it. No doubt it's just the right question to ask!

Women often struggle with issues of looking capable, not understanding what to ask for, or becoming just plain immobilized by what we think will be too difficult. Many of our mothers never dealt with money matters, or better yet, never discussed money with us. That's because their mothers never talked to them either. Even though we were never taught and rarely if ever discussed what to do with money or how to do it, plenty of us suffer the "I should be smarter about this" syndrome, embarrassed about what we don't know or should have done better. We have never built a support system about money matters around us and don't know whom or how to ask for help. And to top it off, things keep changing every day, becoming more and more complicated in the money world.

In truth, you are not really a beginner in the world of money. Only at a very young and innocent age did you know nothing about it. Only at the very beginning of your life did you have no involvement with money. Now, if you are alive, you are connected with money, deeply so. My purpose is to have you acknowledge your participation in your money matters because whether you know it or not, you are your closest and most important adviser.

Again and again, I am touched by the fact that very smart women withhold questions about money for fear of looking ignorant. In doing so, they deny themselves the opportunity to be taken care of and to *get what they want financially.* And I'm not just talking here about a shrinking violet. I'm talking about smart, talented, successful people.

My hope is that through a *human* look at life and money and money and life, we can learn about ourselves, our relationship to money, and the money choices we all must make. If we can identify our relationship to entitlement, responsibility, security, and risk, and can figure out how we handle choices, we can begin to see the direct relationship all these issues have to our money life. I am writing here not just as a financial adviser but as a single mother, a former nurse, whose experience includes interactions about money with family, friends, clients, and of course now you, my readers. I want to use this book to offer the lessons that I have personally learned throughout my life about money and financial decisions, and the lessons other women have shared with me, and then provide you with some down-to-earth possibilities about how we can witness and then change—if need be—our relationship with money.

I think people learn best from other people's stories. The best teachers I ever had told stories from their own lives to illustrate history, sociology, finance, psychology, you name it. Many of the lessons I've learned about life I absorbed at the kitchen table while my mother and grandmother shared their experiences. Storytelling is a legacy we can pass on to others; it is a way to teach and embrace the human element. Over the years I have shared stories of my life and the people I know to make specific points or teach lessons and have found that people not only learn from these anecdotes but they love hearing them. I guess that's why people read novels, to learn about other people's business while we are learning about ourselves. I'm sharing these stories with you so you can learn from all those wonderful people too.

This book is divided into six sections. At the beginning of each section is a questionnaire for you to work on, similar to the one I use in workshops. You may want to copy the pages so that you can reuse the questionnaire in the future. There are no right answers, and no wrong answers, so please be spontaneous in your responses and don't try to answer to please me or get a "perfect" score. Too much thinking will get in your way. These questionnaires are designed to get you to notice where you are *right now* regarding these subjects. Please be candid. Write down your answers before you read the section, as it may be fun to go back and redo your answers in the future and *notice what a difference time and state of mind can make.*

The first section, called ***Before Money Mattered,*** is about how life was in the beginning, the very start. It is an acknowledgment of the process that we used in our early lives to learn about money. You will notice that regardless of which family you grew up in, what town you lived in, you absorbed and developed ideas without conscious intent and that these childhood lessons have been the backbone of many of your adult financial decisions. This section asks you to remember how you began to gather what became the foundation of your money education.

The second section, called ***Entitlement,*** is about what *you* have decided that you deserve in your life. Without using scorecards or comparative measurements, it asks you about what you think you are worth. *You are the one who sets the standards and measures the results.* Until you have decided who you are in the midst of all this money stuff, it will be difficult to seriously take on your financial life.

In section III, ***Responsibility,*** we look without self-judgment but with stark honesty at the issue of responsibility in *our* own money matters. Ultimately we make our own decisions about the role money plays in our lives, so in the end, how things go is our own responsibility.

Section IV is titled ***Security.*** The feeling of being safe, protected, and comfortable is critical to each of us. To deal with money in your life you have to know what makes you feel secure. What makes one person feel secure may not be what another person needs, and because this is such a personal issue, it is important that we understand what makes us act and react to feelings of safety when it comes to money. The chapters in this section are about what happens when people deal with needing a sense of safety. Remember, there is nothing wrong with needing that feeling. It's hard to act to organize your financial life until you've identified what you need in order to feel secure.

Section V is ***Risk.*** Even though some of us get nauseous at the thought of taking risk, literally hate to take it, we all do. We are always risking something, as long as we are breathing in and out. We can't deny it! Risk means taking a chance, putting something at stake.

The important thing here about dealing with risk is that ignorance should never again have to be part of your financial decision making. We need to be conscious, aware, and informed about the risks we're taking, about the kinds of risks out there.

If you follow my logic for a minute, you'll see that once you have decided to figure out what you are entitled to, who in fact is responsible for providing the things you want for yourself, what is important to you in creating the security you desire, and to acknowledge that risk taking is part of life, you will be ready to sink your teeth into the issue of choices.

By the time you have reached the last section, ***Choices,*** I hope you will have learned plenty about yourself. It's not that you haven't always made choices. It's just that now you have the opportunity to look at what you've been choosing and why. Remember, you can change your mind about your choices. *It is your life!*

I.

BEFORE MONEY MATTERED

BEFORE MONEY MATTERED

1. Money is _____.

2. I always feel _____ about money.

3. Having money means _____.

4. If I had a lot of money I would _____.

5. I _____ know what to do about money.

6. Men know _____ about money.

7. When I was growing up, we _____ discussed money or finances.

8. In my family serious financial decisions were made by _____.

9. I feel _____ about my knowledge of money.

10. When I start talking about money and finance, I feel _____.

Before Money Mattered

There was always money;
It just wasn't the same.
It was what grown-ups had,
Coins with a name,

Paper to pay with
For things that were bought—
How did one get money?

That wasn't a thought!

In the Beginning, or Before Money Mattered

When I was growing up, I never thought much about money. There was always enough. Enough for what? Well, enough for food, clothing, rent, and everything else that was important. My father worked two jobs and he never complained. My mother stopped working when I was born and stayed home to take care of us. We made do with what my father earned, and my parents never talked to me or my younger brother about money matters. But somehow we knew how things were.

I knew never to ask for too much. Too much was a pastrami sandwich and French fries at the local deli when we got the treat of eating out. No, I knew to ask for a frankfurter with mustard and sauerkraut. Too much was an entire wardrobe for my Ginny doll, or a new bike instead of the good one that my cousin Sheila had outgrown. I never felt poor, and I certainly never felt rich; somehow, we always had enough.

As I grew older I learned how to pick out wealthy people. No one ever told me. I just learned. For one thing, you could tell them by their clothing. Only wealthy women could afford to wear winter white, while we often dressed in gray, loden green, or navy blue—dark colors that didn't get dirty easily.

People who had a lot of money could have their clothing cleaned more often. They could buy clothes that have to go to the cleaner instead of just throwing laundry in the washing machine. By the time I was eleven or twelve, if I saw a woman who had a winter-white skirt with pleats I knew that she must have had money to burn. After all, pleats were 75 cents extra at the cleaners. In my mind, the cheerleaders were from the families with money. Growing up, I became sensitive to the kinds of things that would and would not be acceptable to ask for, and I knew pleated skirts that had to be cleaned every week were not going to be okay. I was large-chested and self-conscious, so I didn't feel like jumping up and down in a tight sweater anyway; so being financially responsible was a great excuse for not trying out for the cheerleading squad. But that didn't stop me from dreaming that I would grow up and have a closet full of winter-white pleated skirts.

In my home, there was a great respect for the telephone and electric companies and the amount of their monthly bills. Like many children at that time, I never saw or heard of anyone making long-distance calls. Everyone we knew lived close by, and those who moved away either wrote letters or lost touch. When we went on vacation—the farthest we traveled in those days was to the Catskill Mountains and Atlantic City—when we wanted to let friends and relatives know we were safe, we would reach our destination and call home "person-to-person," asking for ourselves or some invented pre-planned name. Whoever answered knew it was his or her job to tell the operator that the person we were asking for wasn't available. Mission accomplished. No wasting words or money. Lengthy, long-distance conversations were for rich people, it seemed to me. Apparently I didn't know any.

The refrigerator in our house also got our respect. Dad said not to open the door and stare at the light, which would waste electricity. Actually, it was during one of those conversations that I first heard about investments and stock ownership. Each time my brother and I lingered at the open refrigerator door, my father asked us if we owned stock in the electric company. As I think about it now, I know that the refrigerator runs whether the door is open or closed. But back then, my father had me convinced that when the light went out the bill went down. Actually, I always thought it would be nice to have stock in these companies so I could use the telephone and open the refrigerator as often as I liked. That's how I decided that rich people have stock. I wasn't really clear how it all worked, but I knew it must be a good thing to have, and you needed to have money to get it.

You may be starting to notice how my mind worked. I had other ways of knowing who had wealth too. I never confirmed these ideas with anyone, I was just sure that they were true ways of measuring affluence.

My Aunt Frances and Uncle Mac lived in a small two-bedroom apartment in the public housing projects on Avenue X in Brooklyn. I didn't know anything about how you got selected to live there; I just knew that they were well-off because their building had an elevator. That was an undeniable determinant of wealth to me. The children on Avenue X had a playground complete with swings, sliding ponds, a jungle gym, and, never to be forgotten, a huge sandbox right in front of the building. Benches allowed the mothers to sit and watch the children play. In the summer the sprinklers would be on all day so kids could cool off. I, on the other hand, lived in a house with no swings, jungle gym, sprinklers, or elevator. I knew that, just like my mother, my Aunt Fran did not work, so I figured that my uncle was a big success at his job, just like my dad. I loved to visit my aunt and uncle. At their house condiments were served at every meal, whereas at our house these were strictly for special occasions. At their house we could even have an entire pickle, while at our house the pickles were cut paper thin. To me the pickles were a dead giveaway that their family had more money than ours. I had no idea that pickles only cost a nickel. I just knew I liked them and that if you could have large quantities of something so rare and special that tasted so good you must be able to afford extravagant things. Not only were there condiments on their table each time I visited, but there were also cakes from Ebinger's Bakery. My mother baked, my aunt bought. I figured out that these boxed blackout and seven-layer cakes were a delicacy and wished we were wealthy so that we could have these same fancy foods at our table. What did I know?

We lived in only two homes during my entire childhood. Until I was 10, we lived in Brownsville, New York. That's where my grandparents had ended up after coming through Ellis Island. Then we moved to a house on East Nineteenth Street where I stayed until the day I got married. For ten years we had the same neighbors, and it seemed to me we also had the same kind of lives. Though it was in fact in Flatbush, Brooklyn, our street could have been any sixties neighborhood. The neighbors were friendly, and knew each other well. All the mothers were housewives; and I never knew or cared what the men did for a living.

Some of my friends had mothers who worked or owned their own businesses. I thought that their moms worked because they had to. I never considered that they might have wanted to. Why would a woman want to work?

There were no family discussions about money. My parents saved their financial discussions for their own private moments, behind closed doors. To this day I have no idea what my dad earned or what they had in savings. I knew that was a conversation not to go near with my mom and dad, that it wasn't my business. It belonged to them and they would take care of things. I was a true innocent, and neither my brother nor I stopped to think about how money worked. Nor did we care. There was enough and there would always be enough, and when our time as grown-ups came, we would somehow know what to do. I had no idea how we'd learn. But don't forget, we were the generation that watched *Father Knows Best* and *Leave It to Beaver*.

You know how things stick with you as you get older? I have strong childhood memories, yet none of them is about specific money conversations. Money was sort of mixed in and hidden with other things. I was always drawing conclusions from inferences and suggestions I picked up in grown-up talk. I deduced the truths about money from the bits and pieces I overheard, and *as I grew up I made life choices based on what I thought was so.* I guess we all do. That's how children have learned for generations—by listening and putting together the pieces of the puzzle.

When I was 10 we moved to a house near Kings Highway, Brooklyn. My old neighborhood was considered poor, and my parents had only paid $36 a month rent. When we moved to our new apartment in 1956 the rent nearly tripled. Of course I didn't know any of this when I was a kid, because adults never talked about these thing around kids. I did notice though that this happened around the time that my dad got a second job. Our new neighborhood had tree-lined streets, excellent schools, and the kids played outside after school with no fear about safety. We even had two bedrooms and a dining room converted to a third bedroom. My bedroom had wallpaper with pink bouquets.

Around that time my grandmother moved in with us. Her real name was Anna but we called her Bubbie Chasha. (You'll hear a lot about Bubbie in this book.) I was her favorite and she was mine and she taught me plenty about life. She came to the United States all alone on a ship from Russia when she was around 16. I say "around," because all the papers burned on the boat after their arrival in New York City, and she never could remember exactly when she was born. She liked it that way. Anyway, she was one of thirteen children, and her father was an orthodox rabbi whose daughters were treated with far less respect than his sons. The girls, for example, weren't allowed to go to school. My grandmother was the youngest in her family and wanted more. One day she announced to her family that she had decided to go to America, where she had heard the streets were paved with gold. She wanted a better life. As it turned out, she never saw her parents again. They were killed by the czar.

When Bubbie came to New York she went to live with distant cousins, much like the immigrants who land at New York's Kennedy Airport do now. She went to work in a "sweatshop," making new suits working long, hard hours. When I sat at the kitchen table taking in her stories, it was Bubbie and my mother who began to instill in me a respect for education and planning ahead. I sat listening to stories about the terrible voyage and the hardships that Bubbie faced with no money and no education.

My grandmother was no fool, especially as she liked to tell it, and she was determined to escape her plight. Like millions of other women, even today, Bubbie thought it would be a good thing to find a man to save her, and so after some weeks of sewing at the factory she went to the local matchmaker and, though she had no dowry, asked that a husband be found for her. And that was how she married Papa Sam. Each era has its own standards, and in those days, at least as Bubbie told it, one sure sign of affluence was girth. There was an assumption that well-fed and well-nourished people were wealthy and healthy. Papa had a job, but he was skinny. Bubbie had no dowry, but she was round. Papa wanted a wife to cook and clean and take care of his needs, and Bubbie wanted a husband so she wouldn't have to work. What a match!

Papa worked the same job as a presser in the garment industry until he died. It was all he knew and all he ever did and it meant that Bubbie never had to go back to work in the sweatshop. It was his job to make the money and her job to make do. They made do and got by and always had just enough. What do *make do, get by,* and *have just enough* mean? I wish my grandmother were still here, so I could ask her to interpret those things for you and me now.

Papa Sam died when he was 65, leaving $1,000 in insurance money and many very sweet memories. Bubbie was only in her fifties, which was too young to collect Social Security, and she had no other income, so my parents took her in. When I was a kid, it was common to have grandparents living in the same house with the rest of their families. There was an assumption that parents would take care of children when they were young and that children would take care of parents when they got older. It was the way I thought things were supposed to be. In those days people made do and life seemed simpler.

It was important to Bubbie that she maintain her sense of independence. Once a week, she would reach into the armoire that held her belongings, pull out an old leather pocketbook, retrieve her blue-covered savings passbook, and march off to the local savings bank. The teller, who knew her by name, would have the amount of interest earned posted on the page and give her her new balance. That little blue book made my grandmother feel safe. It represented all that she had in the world and in truth, in that simpler time, it was all she really needed to know about investing. Later, when she became eligible for Social Security, my parents insisted she keep the money. They knew that having money in her own passbook made her feel secure. Each time a check arrived, she took it immediately to the bank, losing no opportunity to have it earn interest.

Those days are gone. The automatic teller machine, direct deposit, and computerized monthly statements received by mail have replaced the kind of personal relationships my Bubbie and millions of others had with their money. The ways we arrive at learning our values have changed. I saw my grandmother go to the window every month and make a deposit, carefully check her passbook, then put it away for safekeeping. This was like a sacred ritual. Now, even if I choose to put money in a passbook savings account, the banks will pay less interest for the pleasure of having my passbook, and most deposits and withdrawals will take place in a booth where I will place a plastic card in a machine, press some buttons, put an envelope into a steel drawer and if all goes well get a paper receipt confirming the transaction. I don't think Bubbie would have liked that at all.

When my grandmother was alive, we talked about everything under the sun. But never once did we talk about investing money. Some of her sisters were married to prosperous men—I assumed they were prosperous, anyway, from the conversations I overheard. These men had businesses and real estate and they lent people money. We just weren't in their league. In any case, Bubbie's sisters didn't get involved in their husbands' business affairs. Their husbands gave them house money once a week, which was theirs to manage, but everything else concerning finance belonged to the world of my uncles. Bubbie did know some friends who "had money," which I think meant having more money than you needed to live on. These friends invested in stocks when they were young and bonds when they were older, things we knew nothing about, though we did have Christmas club and passbook savings. My grandmother hoped her children would have more than she had ever had . . . and my parents did. In turn, my parents hoped my brother and I would have more than they had, and we do, though I could never imagine how I was going to get where I was supposed to be going. Somehow I guess I thought it would come to me when the time to know came.

Well, the lightning bolt never struck. How could it have? Suffice it to say that I've lived with and tested most of the ideas I formulated about money as I was growing up. Some were dead on and some were deadly. And, all in all, I've gotten to where I am now. I'm sure the same is true for you.

It's too bad that my family didn't have open discussions about money when I was growing up, or that we weren't given classes in school. If you think about it, they do give sex education classes in high school, but with a few exceptions there are no high school money-management classes, even though money has at least as powerful a role in our lives as sex.

The good news is that even if our childhoods have left us ill equipped to meet our adult needs for financial management, money, finance, and investing are learnable, understandable, manageable subjects. What makes money matters complex is that we bring our emotions and historical perceptions along for the ride, dragging with us what we learned growing up, and sometimes that causes us to behave . . . how? Well, mixed-up and confused. You're probably not even aware that often you're using information that was relayed to you by an 8- or 9-year-old child twenty or more years ago when you make decisions now. If nothing else, the world has changed drastically since you made or inherited those assumptions.

Today I'm a financial adviser. I started working with people and their money in 1978. My first career, which lasted ten years was as a registered nurse. As a child I never thought of being anything but a nurse. I certainly never thought my life would follow the path it has. All I wanted was to be a nurse, to wear a blue cape like Sue Barton and Cherry Ames (both nurses in book series for young girls when I was growing up), and take care of people. I started working as a candy striper at local hospitals at the age of 14, as soon as I was eligible to get my working papers. *Ben Casey* and *Dr. Kildare* were prime-time television shows that I watched weekly, never missing an episode unless there was a dire emergency. God, was it exciting. I loved being a nurse. In my mind I was going to work to help pay for the mortgage of the house that my future husband and I would buy. Probably after we had children, I would work on weekends. There was never even a thought of going to medical school. That was for my brother Steve. I never stopped to ask how much money nurses made or what benefits they received. So it shouldn't have come as a shock that my first nursing job in 1966 paid $78 a week, including the differential pay for working from midnight to 8 A.M. I worked for ten days straight, followed by four days off, by which time I was so tired that I slept two days out of the four. I didn't plan to be a primary wage-earner for my family and I didn't really concern myself with money. What I earned was enough for the lifestyle I had back then and that was just fine.

There have been countless changes in my life since then. If someone had told me how my life would unfold, I never would have believed them. No way! I was going to fall in love, get married, have children, and be happy. My career would always be in nursing and I would work part-time to make extra money and keep myself up-to-date. We would make do and get by, put our kids through college, and then we would retire. That's what I expected. That's not what happened. My career, in fact my entire life, changed.

Helping people take care of themselves has been the theme of my adult life. And caretaking can take on different looks. After all, nursing is not so different from taking care of people's finances. You need to follow the same rules: Be careful, be responsible, know the person you are dealing with, don't make assumptions, and read the labels. Don't prescribe anything that has bad side effects. Be sure you know what you are asking someone to take and make sure that it's appropriate for them, whether it's swallowing tablets or handling money.

Make sure they participate in the decision making and make sure they understand that in the end the responsibility about what they choose is theirs; after all, it's their life. And never ever forget that bedside manners matter!

From the caretaker of bodies to the caretaker of finances . . . from keeper of health to keeper of wealth!

In the beginning I never thought much about money. I didn't know then that our relationship with money is critical to our general well-being. I know it now.

Underwear Rules

Listen my children and you
shall hear,
about rules for purchase of
new underwear.

If 16 in April, or 75,
hardly a woman is now alive
who doesn't buy new undies
each year.

Some buy if they date, or
are ready to marry.
Some are quick to the store
while others just tarry!

You've worked hard, you've
played hard,
you deserve a reward.
*You don't stop to think
price . . .
or what you can afford.*

What would your mother
say?
Don't spare the expense.
Purchase of underwear
doesn't make sense.

A promotion, lost weight,
or perhaps
a new baby,
*Good enough reasons for
underwear. . . . maybe.*

Does the voice in your head
determine your pick?
Do you need them or just
want them?
Will they wear out too
quick?

Is the elastic on the waist
sufficiently worn?
You shouldn't wait until the
others are torn!
Do you want red but buy
white?
Do you want silk and
buy cotton?
Look at at how worn out
those old ones have gotten!

Your rules,
not my rules, should
determine your style.
What rules have you made?
Please think for a while.

Underwear Rules

When I was a little girl my Bubbie Chasha used to take me to Washington Baths in Coney Island. My mother stayed home with my baby brother, and I got to go to where the excitement was. Bubbie and her sisters and their children and grandchildren congregated at this big public swimming pool on hot summer days. I can't say that I remember any men. They were either at work or on the handball courts. Men and women were not supposed to do the same things in those days. It was just women and kids. That place was great. We swam, we played, we learned about life!

We used to go early in the morning, by subway. If I close my eyes I can still remember the subway cars. The seats were made of rattan and the cars smelled of the people who traveled in them. The air was thick. Bubbie only allowed me to sit on the side of the car that was closest to the inside track because she thought our weight might cause the car to become unbalanced, tip over, and fall off the overhead El track. I sat where she told me. After all, I was a kid and kids know what they're told; I wasn't about to let the car tip over because of me.

When we got to Coney Island there was an obvious shift in the energy in the air. People actually walked with a bounce in their step, clearly excited to be out in the fresh air, looking forward to a day of sun and sand. We absorbed the sights, sounds, and smells of the space around us, simply enjoying the day. My Bubbie was my friend;

we held hands on these days, talking and sharing our experiences. Bubbie's sisters were all there too. I wasn't the only kid to be accompanied by her grandmother on these trips to Washington Baths. We all sat around eating food we'd brought from home and shared with everyone—eating and talking went on all day. Much of what I know about life I heard there first. As a matter of fact, that was where I first learned about the "underwear rules," from a conversation between Bubbie and her sisters.

It happened like this: Aunt Dora had been scheduled to have some minor surgery the following week. It was a "women's thing." I didn't know what a women's thing was, and I didn't ask. I guess I thought I'd figure it out; that it would unfold from the rest of the story or that in fact it didn't matter anyway. The ladies were discussing her trip to the hospital.

"Did you get new underwear and a robe and slippers, Dora?" somebody asked her.

"Of course! You don't think I know that I'm entitled to get new things for this occasion? Any woman knows that she is at least entitled to new underwear for a time like this."

"Of course you know when to get new underwear. She just asked if you got it," said Bubbie.

Aunt Fannie spoke. "I can't remember the last time I got new underwear. I think it had to have been when my son got married."

"I remember just when I got mine, it was when I went into the hospital to have my last baby," said Cousin Daisy.

"Of course, that's when everybody is entitled to get new underwear," said my Bubbie. "New husbands, new babies, weddings, special occasions, unless of course what you have is falling apart . . . then you can get new ones."

All the women agreed, except for Cousin Sylvia. "I like to give myself a lift every now and then. I get myself a new thing or two. Not just for special occasions, but just as a reward for me from me."

Oops, the ladies were disagreeing on the rules. I needed to listen more carefully.

There was a lull in the conversation. We were passing out food: pot roast sandwiches, hard-boiled eggs, hot tea, and cold Coca-Cola. Not much emphasis was placed on healthy food, at least as we know it now. The emphasis was on having a healthy appetite.

By today's standards these ladies were out of shape, with size 18 or 20½ bodies. (In her heyday, though only five feet two, Bubbie wore a size 40.) But they considered themselves big women, and big was in. It was fashionable. They ate and loved it!

The conversation about underwear rules continued.

"When we were living in Russia, I never thought about this non-sense about when you get new underwear. My mother gave me underwear when she felt it was my turn to get it. I came here and now I'm in charge of buying for me and the children. I only get new underwear when it is worn out." That was my Aunt Dora's neighbor who had joined the talk.

"You mean not even if you have to go to the hospital or for a special occasion?" my Bubbie said in surprise.

"What for? Can anybody see your underwear? In the hospital you take it off; on a special occasion you have other things covering it. I think that it is better to save my money for more important things than an extra pair of bloomers. No matter how much money I have, it wouldn't change my opinion."

"How much is a pair of underwear?" said Aunt Dora. "Why shouldn't I give myself that? I'm glad you don't make the rules for me."

I was getting some very serious information here: these women were talking about life. There wasn't just one set of rules for everyone. This was much more complicated than it appeared to be. What were the true, right rules? Wasn't I going to have to choose for myself one day? I'd better listen carefully! I had to get the rules right.

At the end of the day, after everyone was showered and ready, we would gather our things and head out together toward the subways that would bring us back to our neighborhoods. Sometimes we would stop for an ice cream. The young mothers and the gray-haired grandmas with blue rinses, grandchildren in tow, climbed up the steps to the overhead El. You could smell the salt in the air.

We returned home, where we unpacked and shared the day's events with my mother and father. That was our ritual. I was tired but stimulated, with no desire to go to bed. Bubbie talked about that lady at the beach who didn't even think you were entitled to get new underwear if you were going to the hospital. "Can you imagine? Such funny rules she makes."

My mother could not. My mother thought the same way Bubbie did.

I guess it was then that I had my first realization that people have different *underwear rules.*

What I'd heard that day soon left my conscious mind but somehow stayed with me forever. I was formulating my own underwear rules, though I never thought about them that way.

One day just a while back I was sitting at a pool talking with friends, much like my Bubbie had years before at the Washington Baths. My friend Layne had just ended a relationship and was heartbroken. She had been with her boyfriend for a long time and even though things had been shaky, she had never expected it to end so abruptly. She needed to perk herself up.

"I know what I'm going to do: I'm going to take myself shopping and get myself the best lingerie I can find," Layne said. "After all I've been through, I deserve it. If I'm not entitled to that now, I don't know when I ever will be. It will make me feel sexy and glamorous, and I can sure use all the help I can get on that score."

"I hear you," said Marci. "I think about doing that all the time. I just can't bring myself to spend money on myself in what I consider a frivolous way. It doesn't really have anything to do with how much money I have or don't have. It's just that I have this little voice in my head that questions me: 'Come on, do you really *need* this new Calvin Klein bra, or these expensive silk panties?' "

"Well, if you are not entitled to new underwear after a breakup, when are you?" said Layne.

"If you are having a baby or going to the hospital. And when you get *into* a new relationship."

"Isn't that the truth? How about when you lose or gain lots of weight . . . well, then you have no choice. I also think you're entitled if you get a raise or a bonus," said Jamie.

I remembered my Bubbie and the ladies at Washington Baths. The women I was with now are far removed from their grandmothers' worlds. They are successful, and have their own money and the ability to do whatever they want with it. They are liberated, emancipated, and independent. But they still have underwear rules. So tell me, what's that all about?

Consider that, just maybe, we *are* living by some of the rules that have been handed down to us by our mothers and our mothers' mothers, by our family and neighbors. These rules are a mishmash of everybody else's rules. I know I can trace many of my rules back to

Bubbie and her crowd at the Washington Baths. I'm a financial adviser, and I still find Bubbie's rules creeping into my thinking about money. They always will. She is part of me.

We inherit our underwear rules and then, maybe without ever being consciously aware of it, discard some of them and keep others. And as the years pass we create new ones. Everyone has different rules. They are not necessarily dictated by age, monetary situation, or marital status. Most of us have picked up these rules over time, without even knowing it. They help govern how we live and the choices we make with money. They are part of our heritage.

But no matter how enduring this inheritance is, as adults in today's world we decide *when we are entitled to new underwear,* and by extension, when it's time to begin putting our financial house in order. And as in Bubbie's world, the "underwear rules" we make for ourselves say a lot about *the rules we have created for living our lives.*

II.

ENTITLEMENT

ENTITLEMENT

1. Entitlement means _____.

2. When I feel entitled I _____.

3. I am entitled to _____.

4. Everyone is entitled to _____.

5. Issues of entitlement have shown up in _____ area(s) of life.

6. When I think about money and entitlement I _____.

7. It is _____ for me to say I am entitled.

Entitlement

The subject in question . . . what does it mean?
A birthright? Be selfish?
Act like a queen?
What is the thinking that you have in
your mind?
Deserving and *rewarding* . . . is that what you find?
Each person decides when she is or is not.
Entitlement is a word that stirs up a lot!

Mixed Marriages

Do you know any couples in mixed marriages? How are their lives going? When I said "mixed marriages," I bet you thought I meant simply couples who are of different races or religions. If you really thought I'd stretched the typical definition of mixed marriage, you might have thought I'd included dramatic age differences (say, more than ten years), or perhaps different nationalities. But did you think I'd included couples who are *fiscally challenged*?

When I was dating and thinking about marriage I gave little if any thought to what my beloved felt about child rearing, religion, or money, and I know most of my friends didn't either. We never talked about those things. I can't really recall what we did talk about in those days, though I do remember talking. But I know we didn't talk much about those important subjects. I think we all took for granted that everybody we knew had the same views about how things were and should be, including money, child rearing, and the overall daily dos and don'ts of living.

Don't ask me why I didn't think more about these things. I guess I was too young (19) and inexperienced. It was 1967, and it never even occurred to me that the way I thought about money might not be compatible with the way my husband thought about it. I'm not even sure I knew I had a point of view about money. As I told you earlier, when I was growing up there was almost no discussion of money matters at home. There were conversations about things that cost money, but none about *finances* and ways of handling money. As a result, I assumed much of what I had taken on subconsciously to be the truth, as did my husband-to-be. As it happened, his ideas were very different from mine, and I don't mean different in an enticing or complementary way. They were different with a capital D. We did not know that we were in trouble: in fact we were on a collision course.

My parents paid for our wedding; and my in-laws paid for the band, the liquor, and the flowers. We saved all of our wedding money, my grandmother paid for our bedroom furniture, and friends and family gave us our dishes, pots and pans, and so on. My parents even gave us an old couch of theirs, and my in-laws gave us a secondhand desk and a black Naugahyde chair to complete our living room "suite." We never once talked about saving for a house, for the future, though I assumed that the money we'd received as engagement and wedding gifts would go toward that. Without discussing it, I also thought that everything we earned would go toward that future too.

As it turned out, my husband took a very different view. He felt that we could use our savings to live on, to fill in for what we were not earning. Of course, we had never discussed this; we just assumed the other agreed. Unfortunately both of our names were on the savings and checking accounts, which gave us equal access to the money, whether or not we agreed on what to do with it.

When finally we did start to talk, we discovered we did have similar opinions on religion and child rearing. However, when it came to money we were on opposite ends of the world, and would never even be close in either our habits or opinions. Unknowingly, we had entered into a mixed marriage.

I was a saver; he was a spender. I balanced my checkbook; he never even filled in the numbers on the check register! He believed in buying on credit as often as possible and paying the minimum payment. I only wanted to pay in cash. Owing money made me nervous. My parents had never bought on credit and I was uncomfortable with the concept. I worked as a nurse at the hospital and was guaranteed a paycheck on the first and fifteenth of every month. He was an insurance salesman, working on commission only, never sure of how much he was going to earn. What mattered to me about money was of no concern to my husband, and I in turn thought what he said about it was pure insanity. We weren't just from opposite ends of the world; we were from different planets. How had we missed all of this when we were dating?

I do get it now! In our arrogance and innocence, we assumed that everyone saw the world as we did. They say you can know somebody for years and not really know them at all. But what's still amazing to me is that I didn't know who I was either. I only started to learn who I was when I realized that I didn't agree with my husband. Making financial decisions, struggling to find some middle ground, I came to know more and more about myself and my own relationship to money. It was a journey undertaken with considerable pain and difficulty.

Of course, I thought I was always right and he was always wrong. Isn't that how things go? Didn't everyone know that owing money is wrong? Didn't everyone pay their bills as soon as they got them? Come to think of it, before my husband I'd never even heard of anyone who didn't get a weekly paycheck. I admitted that I'd lived in a relatively small world, but to me that world was reality. And now I was upset. Did I say upset? I felt duped, fooled, and betrayed. How could I have married such a person, somebody with values so different from my own?

Yes, it is true that I should have asked my husband-to-be how commission salespeople got paid, or whether he'd saved anything before our wedding. We should have talked about things like buying on credit, or when and how much to spend on things, and what we considered necessities. Now I realize that in the absence of such a dialogue, we were headed for major problems.

From day one we disagreed about how things should be handled, how much should be spent on birthday and anniversary presents, even how much to spend on a New Year's Eve dinner. Any topic, any conversation had the potential for creating an event. At times these "events" were all-night marathons. When we finally started to talk, I think we'd already been married over a year. Until then, we either fought or skirted the issues or pretended there were no problems. At times we screamed and yelled; at other times we practiced having respectful, listening conversations—talking and talking about respecting each other and how we each viewed money. We tried, but it never worked for us. We were just too different.

We could never create balance and harmony. It went on for years. I complained to my family and friends and he complained to his. I found people to agree with me and he found people to agree with him. I like to say that more people saw things my way, but that did no good because he and I shared the same bank accounts and bills and nobody else's opinion mattered when it came to those.

The marriage ended nine years, two children, and plenty of regret later. I don't blame money entirely, but it certainly took the number one fight-topic spot. And then it began to spill over into every other part of our lives. By then I had started to identify what was important to me and what was negotiable, but we didn't learn to negotiate successfully . . . we had been fiscally challenged, and we had lost.

Being financially challenged as a couple forced us to face plenty of things about ourselves. One thing became crystal clear: *Not all people have the same views of money.* You may think this is a rather simplistic statement, and I guess it is. But most people do not understand it. When entering into a partnership, any partnership, being on the same page financially is essential; being vastly different in this respect can be deadly.

I'll give you another example from my professional life, only this time with a different ending.

By the time my friend Kenny and I started a real estate partnership in Virginia, I was well aware of the potential for trouble as well as for success and prosperity in a partnership. Kenny and I had met a number of years before. He was a lawyer representing someone I had worked with back in my early postnursing days at a company that sold electronic information equipment. My friend John's case involved a broken contract between John and the company. I had been subpoenaed to Washington, D.C., as a witness in the case, having been present at a number of meetings where contract negotiations had taken place. Expecting a day trip, I had packed only a dress and one pair of panty hose. Unfortunately the judge had other ideas and I ended up staying the entire duration of the trial, four days. It was a rough four days. My boys were still young and were very unhappy that I had left them for so long; my baby-sitter, not pleased with the development, was shaking her head; and I was completely unprepared, with my one outfit and new panty hose. But as it turned out, I met a lot of interesting people. That's where Kenny and I started our friendship.

At the time we designed our business venture we were both divorced, he had started his own law practice, and I had recently become a financial adviser. Each of us had thought about how we would like to secure our financial futures. Neither of us had much money. I lived in New York and he lived in Richmond, Virginia. The great idea we had in common was that we would buy and develop real estate in Richmond, in particular in an area called the Shokoe Bottom, which was known for a so-called 100-year flood that showed up every five years or so. Because of the flood there had not been much interest in developing this property for a long time, but Ken had heard that the city was building a flood wall, which would obviously improve the value of the location. This made it an extraordinary opportunity for two people with a small amount of money to invest.

At that time Leona Helmsley still was known as the Queen of Real Estate; *60 Minutes* had just run a special show about her and her life with her husband, Harry. I admired Leona Helmsley then, and wanted to be just like her. Well, not in every way, but I did dream of having a large real estate empire and making lots of money. So did Kenny. Ours seemed like a perfect match. Even so, we talked endlessly to clear up any misconceptions, knowing that this could be a big opportunity and we couldn't afford to blow it. What did he consider risk? What did I? What did he consider safe? Did I agree? Did we trust each other? What were our weaknesses and our strengths? Could we avoid the hazards of a financially mixed marriage? Would we have a financial meeting of the minds?

Like me, Ken was recently divorced, and the financial differences in his marriage had proved disastrous too. Both of us were hell-bent on putting our hard-won lessons to good use. By this point we had been friends for a while, but our friendship had nothing to do with money, and now money was going to be at the cornerstone of our partnership. No matter what we thought we knew about each other in the beginning, we had to keep redefining things as time progressed. At least we were both heading up the same road. As much as we thought we knew each other, we were surprised at how much work it took us to stay clear and understand each other.

Our partnership continues to this day. We don't always agree. Sometimes we have to negotiate with each other and meet in the middle. Sometimes one of us bows to the other's experience, expertise, or just plain feelings about the matter. It depends. We have both matured over the years. We have had to redefine our goals and objectives and interpretation of what the words "long-term" and "cash flow" mean. Even though our approaches are similar they are not identical, which means we are always working things through. That makes all the difference for us. As far as the investment is concerned, the flood wall was built and the Shokoe Bottom has been growing ever since. We went through some rough times in the late eighties, and learned plenty about the risks of real estate investment. Overall, I credit the success of our partnership to our strong friendship and the fact that we were clear in our communication with each other from day one.

The more complex our lives become—the more choices about where and what and how we can do things with money—the more closely we need to look at our personal preferences and differences. In recent years we have been given more investment choices, which creates more room for disagreeing as well as more ways of borrowing and more ways of spending. Take the **adjustable rate mortgage,** for example. I'm sure you know people who like the fact that their mortgage rate is not locked in. Perhaps you have even considered using an adjustable rate yourself, or are already using one. Someone who uses this kind of mortgage must feel comfortable with the idea that after a fixed period of time—it could be months, or years—the rate they pay will change as interest rates change. These people don't mind that in exchange for paying lower rates now, they must live with the risk that rates will go up and they may have to pay more in the future. Usually an adjustable rate mortgage is offered at an initially lower rate, which the borrower enjoys until the anniversary date of the mortgage comes due. That's one reason some people like it. They are willing to deal with the future in the future. On the other hand, what if you are in a mixed marriage and your spouse can't stand to live with that kind of uncertainty? What if he or she needs to know *now* and for the next thirty years exactly what the mortgage payment is going to be? As I'm sure you've already guessed, we have a potential sore spot here. Is there a right answer? And if there is, the right answer for whom?

Just as you thought you'd solved that one here comes the home equity loan, which makes it possible to get a loan from banks using our homes as collateral. Another term for **home equity loan** is **second mortgage.** This rate may not be fixed, and you can pay it down as fast as you like. So if the value of your house goes up, you will be able to take out some of the profits in the way of a loan. But the debt from the loan is paid down month by month . . . which means your fixed monthly expenses go up. It's true that you will get a tax deduction from the government for the interest you pay on the loan, which may make it begin to seem like a perfectly great idea. Maybe your accountant even suggested it. If so, it must be a sound move, right? After all, the house has built equity and the second mortgage is a way of getting money from the house without selling it. You probably never expected you could use your home to finance a new car, or boat, or perhaps your child's education, and this gives you a very positive outlook about the economy and the future. But one person's rosy future is another's financial nightmare. Let's say your spouse doesn't want to take on more debt. He wants to downsize. You want to live a little. Your partner puts his foot down. That's it. What then?

Or how about investing in the stock market? What happens when you can't bear the thought of any loss of principal but your significant other believes in taking risk and betting that the future will be just like the past, i.e., secure and successful. Maybe your partner's family always invested in high-quality stocks and had good experiences. Why should the future be any different? Asking someone who is terrified of losing any principal to make this kind of investment is like asking them to put their finger in a socket. If your partner believes that putting all your money in the bank is a deadly (conservative) sin, your fear of loss may seem ridiculous and confining. You may have a nervous stomach about losing money, and your partner may feel ill at the prospect of losing an opportunity.

And then there's always the matter of credit cards and borrowing. Some people believe in leverage, in using all possible money available. They are excited about the concept of putting down 10 percent on a real estate investment and taking a mortgage for the rest; or borrowing 50 percent (margin debt on an investment account), buying twice the amount of stocks or bonds they could ordinarily afford. They see these things as an opportunity, if the investment goes well, to make higher returns because of the increased amount of money at risk. It seems as though they don't stop to consider that if the investment is a poor one it is also an opportunity to lose big. They are willing to take chances that seem outrageous and unacceptable to their partners. Some people literally gag at this thought.

Let's say you don't have the money now, but you will next month after your bonus check, and you don't want to miss the opportunity of buying the stereo on sale. He doesn't want anything that he can't afford, right here and now. You have the credit card available and the bill doesn't even come for another three weeks. What's his problem? You! Oh, well!

Or, consider buying versus leasing a car. Do you want to have the car be yours from day one; does paying all that money and having nothing to show for it at the end bother you? Or are you the one who says, "Let's lease; that way we put little or no money down. We're not going to keep the car forever anyway. This way we can decide at the end of the lease." Can you see the wall come up? You are now on opposing sides and the war is on.

What about the children? Spending money on the children is a beauty. Private or public school for the kids is always a great conversation piece for a mixed-marriage couple.

Have either of you ever inherited money? For couples caught on the mixed-marriage merry-go-round, this one is a doozy. How should one spend an inheritance? And always complicating the situation is the fact that the money is usually left by one side of the family, one parent or aunt or uncle on one side of the family. Even if the money is left to you both, we know it really is the bounty delivered from "your" family. And if it comes from your family, you should have more of a say if there is a difference of opinion, shouldn't you? The saver wants the money in the bank, the spender wants to remodel the kitchen or garage—or how about that trip that you've never taken? Is this extra money that you would never, ever have had and feel you should enjoy, or do you consider this a once-in-a-lifetime opportunity to sock away some savings?

On a smaller scale, should you buy no-name brands or go for the higher-costing brand name? He doesn't mind using one-ply bathroom tissue; her values wouldn't allow anything but two-ply. Sound silly? Maybe, but in mixed marriages, the silly things can get serious all too easily.

You may be smiling right now. You may be thinking that no two people can agree about everything, that differences are unavoidable. Yes, of course I agree. However, it is the degree of difference that can cost us dearly. A disagreement may seem minor, but scratch the surface, and you may find a yawning chasm.

Mixed marriages *can* work, but they require special skills. You have been fiscally and financially challenged. Everyone wants to be right! When it comes to money, some things are generally universally right, but many, many things are "right" just because of who we are and how we think things ought to be.

Living in a mixed marriage will require empathy and compassion at a level that you may have never been called on to employ before. Take inventory for yourself and determine what is critical for you about money matters and what is open for discussion. Look at your relationship to entitlement, responsibility, security, and risk and try to determine where you and your partner are the same and where you are different. Be honest with each other.

Money Attitude Inventory

1. Do I consider myself a spender or a saver?
2. Do I prefer to risk return, safety, or opportunity?
3. Am I willing to lose some of my money?
4. If I am willing to risk losing some . . . how much is some?
5. Am I willing to go into debt and, if so, what kind of debt (home, car, investments, credit card)?
6. Am I comfortable with where my investments currently are?
7. What return would I be satisfied with on my investments?
8. Do I feel positive about the future financially?
9. Is everything negotiable? What is not?

Share your answers with each other. There's no time like the present to get clear about the issues at hand. Spend enough time speaking to your financial advisers so that you can get the best picture possible of how you can make your financial life work, still allowing for your differences. *Honesty is critical in the true light of day when two people from two different money worlds try to make it on Planet Earth together.*

You may want to consider having separate investment accounts and individual credit cards. Sometimes that's not enough and problems arise anyway about "my money and yours," but it may be a good place to start.

Pam and Joel ran a restaurant that they bought together. They were sure that nothing could get in the way of their love for each other, but they were wrong—something did. It was their budget for marketing, and deciding how much and where to spend their money that drove them crazy. Joel wanted to expand rapidly and be aggressive with the money they spent on local advertising. It made Pam very nervous. They struggled with financial issues constantly and finally decided that the best solution was to open another restaurant. Pam would run one and Joel would run the other. They would be partners in both businesses but have independent decision making for each store. Their arrangement seems to be working. Now, you may think that's pretty extreme, but it was what they needed to do to keep their sanity and their marriage intact. Both restaurants are doing well—and so are Pam and Joel!

There are times when we are willing to negotiate and change about some issues and not about others. Just be clear what they are. I love to buy things for my grandchildren. Sometimes the things are frivolous, but I don't care because it makes me happy to buy them. Last year I had stars named after both my grandchildren, Tiana and Tyler. There is a group called the International Star Registry, based in London, that officially names stars for people. Now and forever they are inscribed in the heavens and I find it a wonderful concept that through this act I have created a kind of immortality for them. Each of these stars cost $75. For this money they not only got stars named after them, they got a map of the constellations and the place where the stars have been identified in the galaxy. These little maps gave my entire family great pleasure. We had the certificates framed to hang in the kids' room.

I'm a sucker for mushy, romantic things, and when it comes to my kids and grandchildren it gives me great pleasure to do that kind of buying. It would make me very unhappy to have a partner who disapproved and disagreed every time I went and bought gifts for my babies, especially the froufrou kind. Even if you don't do it yourself, I'll bet you know someone just like me. I am more than willing to negotiate about where to eat and how much to spend, which car to buy and what stocks to own. I do not want to discuss what I give to the kids; not those kinds of things. That is mine to decide. Hey, don't you have your own special things?

If you are already in a fiscally challenged marriage, and you are upset and frustrated, you really need to practice compassion and empathy. *You can bet that your partner is in a similar place, just at the opposite end of the spectrum.* Try to explain to your mate not only *what you feel* about money issues but also *how it makes you feel.* Use the Money Attitude Inventory alone or with your partner, and share your answers. Try to find some common ground to operate from. It is possible.

Money is a powerful teacher. It is an inescapable part of everyday existence and it can give you the opportunity to know yourself and your partner. As in the rest of your life, the best tools for making this partnership-in-money work are honesty, compassion, and an acceptance of the fact that people are not always the same in their thinking. This is different from questions of right and wrong, better or worse. It's more like right and left, short and tall, man and woman. *Different!*

Intention! Intention!

You know how you live a certain way because that's the way that you think it's supposed to be? Some place in your growing up you learned lessons and they just stuck. It wasn't as if my parents sat me down and taught me about intention or commitment or stick-to-itiveness. They were just lessons I learned along the way with a host of others. One of the best ones goes as follows: *INTENTION is more than 50 percent responsible for getting us to our goals.* It is *Intention* that gives us the ability to hang in no matter what, that can be the difference between success and failure.

In the world of money, intention holds the number one spot on my list of things that matter. I've seen it at work!!

When I was 29, my husband and I separated; we were divorced one year later. My boys, Jonathan and Andrew, were 6 and 3 at the time. It wasn't our first separation; once before we'd been separated for a year and gotten back together for a short time. For the sake of the boys, the family, and all of the usual good reasons we'd tried to make a go of it and for a host of other reasons that in the end made more sense, the marriage didn't work.

Although money mattered and in fact was a major issue in my marriage, it was only when we decided to divorce that for the first time money became a real focal point in my life. Now it was really *my money.* It was during that time that I began to take ownership of the money in my life, crossing what I call the Bridge of Intention.

What happened to me about money happens to most of us at

one point or another. It is that "ah-ha" moment that finds us saying, "Oh well, I guess it's up to me, really up to me."

At the time of my divorce I was working as a nurse at the local hospital earning $136 a week doing per diem work. That rate was the highest I could get at the time, and in order to get it, I had to forgo any benefits such as health insurance or pension. Those things were so out of my reality that it didn't matter anyway. What did matter was that I was locked in to the job I had and to a fixed income. I had to work until eleven at night or leave the house at five in the morning so that I could be home by four in the afternoon when the boys got home from school. I began to see that being a nurse wasn't going to make it for me any longer.

I thought about my life and all the changes I was facing, and I was really scared. I wanted more income and more personal freedom. In those days there was no way that as a nurse I could take time off to go to open-school day and see my kids' school play. In those days you weren't even allowed to receive a personal call when you were on duty.

So it seemed very reasonable to think of leaving nursing, even essential. I decided I'd get a job in sales. To me, sales seemed to hold a lot of the answers. I figured I would just go out and get a job working for a pharmaceutical company, visiting doctors' offices and telling them to write prescriptions for the products of the company I was working for. They would be thrilled with me and with the stories of the medical breakthroughs I would share with them. Only, as it turned out, there just weren't any jobs in the New York City area for ex-nurses who wanted to work in sales. I guess everyone else had the same idea. In any case, all the pharmaceutical companies who were hiring were based in New Jersey and wanted people who lived near them. I wasn't about to move from Whitestone, Queens, all the way to New Jersey.

Instead, I got a job working for a company that sold outdoor and indoor electronic information-display equipment. That's right, I sold things like electronic scoreboards, time and temperature clocks, and even helped sell that great big four-color sign that for years hung on Broadway and Forty-second Street that everyone has seen on New Year's Eve when the ball drops. The company I worked for was based in Spokane, Washington, and I wanted to work for them because my compensation included a base salary of $12,000, use of a company car, and my home telephone. I also wanted them because I could come and go to and from my home and my boys without answering to anyone. All they were interested in was the results of my sales. They chose me because they hadn't really been able to break into the New York market and hoped that hiring a woman to work in what had been historically a man's business would help. Frankly, as I look back on it I can't figure out what possessed them to hire me; it must have been destiny, the hand of the gods. A marriage was made.

I was clueless about what I was getting into when I was sent to a small town in Connecticut for one week to learn how to be a district sales engineer, but my heart was set on making it. During this time I was taught to knock on doors, create interest, deliver a presentation, and close the deal. The art department provided fine renderings that I would use in my presentations to the bank or other business interested in our equipment, to show them how much good will and fine advertising our time and temperature clocks would provide. Whenever the potential client asked about how things operated, I was told to tell them, "Don't worry, we'll black box it." Apparently, that was a technical expression, but I had no idea then and have no idea to this day what it meant. I thought it probably referred to the wiring and electrical workings, but I didn't ask. I don't know why, but the answer seemed reasonable enough to me. In any case my clients always nodded in agreement when I gave them that answer, which meant that either they knew what it meant or they didn't want to look uninformed either. I was off and running with my new career.

I was clear in my intention. I was going to make money, and have a way to spend some time at home with my boys if I needed to. I got just the kind of job that I needed to make this happen.

My territory was New York City, including Staten Island. There were already a number of small savings institutions that had our fine, high-caliber time and temperature clocks, which made it easier to go back to them and sell additional signs for the new branches they were opening; they already knew the value of our displays. So when I heard that one of the banks was opening yet another branch, I was delighted, and off I went to make a presentation to the bank president. With my trusty Polaroid camera in tow, I visited the site of the new branch, took pictures, came back with my beautiful art renderings, and sat down with the bank architect and the bank president to discuss the location of the sign. "Where shall we put the sign?" asked Mr. President. "Here," I said, pointing at a spot in the front of the building. "I'm not sure; it may not work there," said the architect. "Well, she's a district sales engineer and this is her business," said Mr. President. The architect sighed. "You may be sorry." We made plans to install the sign right in front of the building just in time for the grand opening. I was delighted. And then spring came and a weeping willow tree began to bloom and our beautiful sign was obliterated. So much for the opinion of the district sales engineer!

I called the sign company and we made arrangements to move the time and temperature clock at a nominal fee. This happened in 1976 and I'll always remember it. The architect had been right. The lesson I learned was one I won't forget, which was that we can't always see what will be showing up in our future. It's best to try to plan ahead and ask plenty of questions. (And what's a district sales engineer, anyway? It's always best to find out what a title really means too!)

The sign company and I parted ways two years later, in 1977. You see, I had won a contest sponsored to produce competition among all the sales engineers. The prize was a trip to London and Paris, and the brochure read: "Win a trip to Europe for you and your wife." Surely they had forgotten about me when they designed that thing, which made me determined to win; there was no question about it. I was already way ahead of the "other men," so when I won I wasn't surprised. But management was. And they wouldn't let me take a man, even though I was a young, single (newly divorced, you should pardon the expression) woman. They were afraid the wives wouldn't like that. I didn't even think about my legal rights. They wouldn't give me the cash for the trip, and they wouldn't let me bring a man. They wouldn't even give me the cash value of the second trip that I had won for my "wife."

When you are feeling poor, are newly divorced, and have just won a great trip, you get very excited about having an opportunity to go someplace special. I really wanted to go, and was therefore committed to finding a solution. The solution turned out to be my friend Louise: she came with me, paying her portion of the taxes that would be due on the trip. Off we went, and we had a great time. I quit right after we got back.

•   •   •

I knew I could sell. That had been made clear to me when I was a young nurse, able to get a 200-pound man to swallow castor oil and orange juice. I could sell anything! Now I had worked in sales and had been proven right; I had been a success at my job selling outdoor electronic information-display equipment, "black boxed" or not. I had even won a trip to Europe. I was soon hired by some friends, psychologists who had created an innovative method for sales and management training and were selling their programs to banks and brokerage houses. They paid me $20,000 a year and gave me a car too. I was becoming positively sophisticated.

Now it happened that every time I went to a brokerage firm to talk about what our training programs could do for the prospective client and how valuable they were, some manager would suggest that I become a financial adviser. "You have all the tickets—you're bright, people like you, and you have a good attitude; besides, you have two boys to support," they would say. "No thanks," I would say.

But one day, after about a year and a half in this job, I woke up and thought, I'm making $20,000. I'm supporting two children almost alone and I'm 30 years old. I might just keep going along this way and get too comfortable or just too scared and if I don't step up to the plate now, I may never have the courage.

I wanted to work for myself, but I was also terrified. If I stayed where I was I would stop growing, but if I left I could lose all the security I had. The people I worked with were wonderful; they cared about me, but this didn't detract from the fact that I was limited: by the amount I could earn, by what I could learn, and by the scope of my position and the potential input I could have. If I changed now I was going to be putting myself in the world of the BIG BOYS. In the journal I kept I wrote: "Sometimes I'm afraid I'll get too comfortable and I won't push forward. If I move ahead I could fail but if I stay where I am I may not grow and that scares me even more."

My intention was to be successful and to control my own destiny. My intention was to be independent. That last consideration made my decision for me. I would only be paid what I earned. There would be no salary, no guarantee, no promises. I was going to make that call. I was going to ask for the opportunity to become a financial adviser. Whew!

When I was married I had thought that no matter what my career was it was my husband's job to be the primary breadwinner. I had picked up that idea from looking at how everyone around me had behaved when I was growing up. Where else but to my closest family, friends, and the television set could I have looked for guidance? But now money mattered in a different way, and I was determined to take on what I knew would be one of the biggest challenges of my life. I was going to be in charge not only of my money, but of money that belonged to other people too.

The day after I came to my decision I made a call to one of the managers I knew. David had said before that he would like to hire me. He was a very smart and interesting man, and the thought of working with him appealed to me. He wasn't in his office when I called but his secretary knew me well and she told me how to find him. I immediately phoned him in Washington, D.C., where he was visiting another branch. When I make up my mind to get something done, I let very little stand in my way.

When I called Washington, I was told that the manager in question was in an important meeting, but he called me back during his break. "I need to see you right away," I said. I think he thought I was asking for a date. Don't forget that this was the late 1970s. "Well, I'm on my way back to New York tonight, but I leave for Boston right after that and won't be available for a week. I'm flattered that you called, but can't we have dinner next week?"

He didn't understand my intentions, that all I was looking for was a job interview, and I didn't try to explain. Instead I suggested, "I'll pick you up at the airport tonight when you arrive and drive you into the city. What flight are you on?" We met at La Guardia Airport, where I handed him the keys to my car. It was pouring out, and gales of wind were pushing us. "You drive," I said, "I'll talk." He drove, I talked. The trip took longer than usual because of the nasty weather, which was good as far as I was concerned.

I explained that I had decided to take him up on his offer to join the Wall Street elite, that I was ready to take the plunge, to go for it. I had become clear on this and I wanted to explain my intentions to him. I could give my current employer notice and start in two or three weeks. He was shocked. "Well, you know you have to take some exams, take a psychological profile as well as a math aptitude test. I can make arrangements when I return next week. When I get back from Boston we can talk again."

I wasn't having it. I'd made up my mind and I was going to Wall

Street. Probably my grandmother felt the same way when she became clear that she was coming to America. It was time for change. Caretaking was what I did best and I'd decided to do it with money. Now everybody's money would matter, and I was ready to go. "Make arrangements for me to take the exams tomorrow so the results will be ready by the time you get back," I told him. And, bless that sweet man, he did.

I took the exam and thought all night about the risk I was about to undertake. I was totally responsible for the outcome of my life. I had never had such a focus before. This would be the very first time in my working experience that I'd only get as much money as I earned. I had two children, and they needed me to win. Plenty of people would be putting their faith in me with their money, and I certainly wanted them to win. I was committed to winning. Talk about intention!

After waiting a few days for David to call me, I couldn't wait anymore so I called him to set up an appointment to discuss the results of my exam. I was anxious to get moving. Don't think that I wasn't also scared to death—I was, but nothing could stop me now.

The math and English results were great. The psychological testing company had stamped my exam "Strong Hire Recommendation." But, as I saw the half-glasses slip down David's nose while he looked down at the shoeshine he had just gotten, something told me that we weren't going to cut a deal that day. My belly began to knot up. Something was lurking in the sidelines and I couldn't figure out what it was. Then he explained, "You see, Eileen, I don't have a desk for you to sit at just now. If you can hold on until September"—it was now May—"when we move I will have plenty of space to bring you on. You surprised me. I didn't think you'd be in such a rush to get things started." He also probably didn't think I'd be that good. The results of the exams were there in black and white, but he was still looking for reasons to wait.

Don't ask me what possessed me at that moment. I've thought about it more than a couple of times myself. I just told David that there was no way that I could wait now. First of all it would be dishonest to my current employer. When you're in a sales position and you know you're going to leave, you just don't have your heart in setting up any future business that you know that you are not going to be there to do. That much David understood. I had made the decision to leave and now I was going to do just that. But I also now had evidence, in writing, that I was a good candidate for hiring by a brokerage or financial services firm, and I would go to someone else who was ready to hire me if he wasn't able to do something right away. I suggested that I would much prefer to work for him (which was the truth), and that I knew that because I would be studying for my exam as the first part of my training and because new trainees need to have been employed by a firm for at least three months before they can take the license examination required by the Securities and Exchange Commission, we would have to be creative. I suggested that I stay at home to study for the upcoming exam, just as I would if I were coming in every day to participate in the training program. He could even mail me my paycheck. This would solve both of our problems. I could hardly believe it myself, but he agreed. Since I had ad-libbed this whole thing without giving a thought to whether anyone had ever done this before, I had no idea how unusual my suggestion was. Had I known that the answer would normally have been no, I might not have asked in the first place. I didn't know not to ask. But my extraordinary sales pitch had also shown him that I was strong-willed, very responsible, and had a strong intention to succeed.

The mailman delivered my paycheck every week. I stayed home and studied. I studied at the beach, in my living room. I studied all the time. It was like studying a foreign language.

Each night I wrote in my journal. I felt like I was in the twilight zone. Even the tangible paychecks didn't quell my anxiety because I was afraid that with all my good intentions to have this turn out well it still might not. I was afraid that one day I would wake up and my dream would end. But, I kept studying and planning and getting ready, until finally September came and I was ready to take my exam. I passed, and then the week after Labor Day I started to work on Wall Street.

It's Never About
the Money

It's never about the money. Money is only an instrument that we use to play out all the private conversations we have in life about things like worthiness, power, security, risk, and on and on and on. The story I'm about to tell you will point out what we already know about ourselves anyway: human beings are very complicated. Complicated and smart. So smart sometimes that we even fool ourselves about what we are really up to, what we are really creating around us. I think that money is a metaphor, and that if we are willing to look at that as a possibility, we can learn an awful lot about ourselves and what we are *really* up to, what we *really* think we deserve, what we *really* want.

A long time ago I met a wonderful woman named Sarah Winsome. She was an up-and-coming writer, had great wit, and was great fun to be with. We hung out together. On warm summer nights we would talk about the time when all of our dreams would come true, when we would have plenty of money (whatever that meant), fame, and success. I had been working as a financial adviser for about ten years by then and Sarah worked as a copy editor. Neither of us was rich yet, but we could see the possibility of making very substantial incomes in the future, and more than that, being respected for our work. Sarah made around $20,000 a year, with health insurance and two weeks' paid vacation. But her dream was to be independent, to create, and to be successful.

Sarah led a simple life. When she was a very young child, her family had come here from Trinidad and worked as domestic help for wealthy people in Manhattan. She was a graduate of public schools and the state university. She was taught to live in mediocre surroundings, have mediocre clothing, and expect very little from other people. You could tell that she was used to living on small sums. She was very frugal. Both her parents had died when she was in her early teens and her remaining family was a sister, with whom Sarah had a very strained relationship. Sarah says that they had fought for years over their mother's attention—there was so little of her to get, because she was always working—and their childish sibling squabbles persisted into adulthood. Sarah had a very strong network of friends who rooted for her success and just knew in their hearts that she would be the one neighborhood sister to make it out on her own. For them, she was the dream, the hope, the ticket out.

All Sarah wanted was to be an accomplished writer. To be accepted for her talent was the pot of gold at the end of the rainbow. She wasn't interested in finding a man to take her out; she was writing her own ticket. And then, one day, it happened. She won national acclaim. Her first book got her the acknowledgment she desired as well as enough money so that she could retire from copy editing. Suddenly, there she was, valise in hand at a writers' colony in a small town just outside of Cape Cod, ready to do what she loved best: write. She was working on her first novel. She'd quit her nine-to-five job, sublet her studio apartment, and was off to write her heart out, to be where she truly belonged . . . and so it was.

That was ten years ago. Sarah has "made it." I'm proud to report that she has a retirement plan that she diligently funds every year, now worth well into six figures, and a personal investment account. She travels and she writes. She is involved in a committed, loving relationship, and her work is highly respected all over the world. The dilemma for Sarah now is that the money she has earned seems to have created a lot of upset. She had never anticipated that there would be problems associated with financial success. It seemed that success and money would be the answer to her prayers. I know that just about now some of you are thinking that you should have her problems! No kidding—success, respect, love, and money, what's the problem? Even I can go along with that.

But when Sarah started making money, her cousins, neighbors, and old friends from the neighborhood were very impressed. They also started reaching out to her for assistance. So did Sarah's sister. Everybody had an idea about how they could start a great business if they just had some seed money. Everybody knew of a piece of property out of the old neighborhood that they could buy for a song. It was hard for her to say no. After all, how can you say no to people who are part of your history, to the very people who had always believed in you? Weren't they entitled to a piece of her success? The money started to represent how she was different from them, to make her feel separate.

So, in the beginning there were lots of loans that she knew would never come back to her but that she made anyway because she wanted to let these folks know that she remembered her roots and that she would never forget them. After she returned from the writers' colony, and in fact throughout her early career as an independent writer, she continued to live in her tiny apartment, and to shop in the local stores. The comfort she took in belonging overrode her need to expand financially. And she said that, anyway, you can't always bet on being able to sell every new book you write. She talked about taking a job at the state university that would provide a pension and health insurance. At least it was good to know that the possibility was there to fall back on if the need arose.

Sarah's old friends let her know that they felt she was growing away from them. Her sister in particular was angry that she was not privy to all Sarah's business, nor a partner in any venture. Sarah was dealing with agents, accountants, attorneys, and even press agents, and most of this wasn't fun. She had not been brought up in a world where dealing with power and money was part of the usual routine. She felt strange and apart from everybody, without a strong connection to either her old world or her new one.

Talk about being torn. And what made it especially difficult for our girl was that she *knew* that this wasn't just about the money. Part of her wanted to move out of the old neighborhood, to buy an apartment; the other part of her was afraid. Part of her wanted to share everything that she had with everybody who didn't have as much, while the other part of her felt increasingly ripped off by her sister and friends. Her fantasy was that she could just walk away from making any decisions about any of these matters, to abdicate responsibility. "No more, thank you very much, I just don't want to deal with any of this anymore." The problem was that she didn't know what was fair, what she was really entitled to. She thought maybe somebody else could decide this. She discussed nothing with her boyfriend, from whom she wanted to shield knowledge of her finances. She worried that his interest in her might be based on her money. She went to Europe for eight months to write a second book and when she came back all of her money issues were right there waiting for her return.

Her life was in her face. For Sarah, as for many of us, making decisions and standing up responsibly for those decisions has powerful overtones. Even though we say we want lots of things in our lives, sometimes we don't act in ways that would make that happen.

Her boyfriend wanted to get married, but he was willing to just live together first if that would make Sarah happy. But nothing was making Sarah happy these days. They had been seeing each other almost four years, and up until now Sarah had felt that as long as each of them still had their own apartment and were locked into their leases nothing could threaten the status quo, a status quo Sarah liked and needed. She liked having him and still being single. It was safe. She wasn't sure she would make a good wife, and became uncomfortable with all the wonderful things he was offering. Now, all of a sudden, when they began to talk about sharing a place the question at hand became more than whether to buy real estate. Both of them had money, so scarcity couldn't be used as an excuse anymore. Sarah was feeling trapped and she wasn't sure what was really bothering her.

Sarah gave power of attorney to her lawyer and her accountant so that she never needed to sign any documents or papers if she didn't want to. They could do it for her. If she did decide to buy an apartment and things didn't work out, it could be someone else's fault. Of course, this arrangement had the potential to produce a cascade of new problems and issues—and it did. Sarah was really getting upset. She felt that agreeing to buy an apartment would then lead to discussions of marriage. She had felt so much safer before. They would have to furnish a home. With all these new bills and financial commitments would come the need for homeowner's insurance, and disability insurance in case she should become ill and not be able to write: if you are sick and can't write you don't get paid—better get disability insurance. Then there was a new book contract. There would always have to be another book if there were going to be bills like these. But shopping for furniture would take time away from her writing, not to mention that with all the overhead, writing was becoming a pressure, a thing she had to do. It was no longer a matter of wanting to create; she was obligated to create. She couldn't depend on her boyfriend's ability to make money, because he was a writer too. What if she was no longer any good at writing? What if she did take the risk of getting married and her marriage failed, as her parents' had? What if she didn't fit into the new neighborhood? Her anxiety level was rising, and things were getting out of hand.

The money in her life began to represent all the nightmares and fears from her childhood that she had hoped she had left behind by this point. She was feeling lonely and frightened, when all she had ever wanted was to be happy. But now she wasn't happy at all, and it seemed there was no escape. And so we talked.

Obviously, there was no point in Sarah's getting everyone to take power of attorney for her. She was getting calls anyway and decisions still had to be made. Besides, all her advisers knew each other and knew that she felt that everything was a hot potato and she didn't want to be the one holding it. But there was no getting around the fact that it was *her* hot potato. The apartment didn't need to become a commitment to marriage unless she wanted it to. In fact, she didn't need to buy an apartment; she could rent alone in another place. Or, she could rent with her boyfriend in a place that they could share and then see about buying. It was she who was choosing to act out in this way, even while there were other ways of handling things. Nobody in her family had ever had to deal with these issues. Success was new to the Winsome family, and she was the crusader taking on new territory.

Now she was also the one who had to be willing to say that she *deserved* to move into a new apartment with or without a man, to have beautiful furnishings, and not apologize for being successful. It was up to her to choose the lifestyle that suited her, not to look to other people to choose it for her. A person can't run far enough or fast enough or long enough to avoid such choices. You have to make your own decisions about how you will live your life, and ultimately, you have to be ready to take responsibility for what is happening, or pay the price for giving up your power.

Sarah finally started to realize that the success and money that had come into her life were not the real problems she was experiencing. She just had never been prepared for what might happen to her when they came her way. She was overwhelmed by important choices, and saddened by the feeling that she had to apologize to old friends and family for her new life. She had wanted to run away and now realized she couldn't. This was all very painful, and certainly not how she had imagined it would be. She had thought that life would be simple, that things would simply unfold. But things don't just unfold, and she was discovering that we create and choose and pattern how things happen.

Sarah made a decision to buy her own apartment. Her boyfriend could move in with her and help share the bills, but she wanted her own place for now. She didn't want to get married just yet and was afraid to tell him, but she did. He didn't move in with her for a couple of months, but he did help her decorate the place. That was over a year ago. Now they are talking about getting married, when she feels ready.

She has also told her attorney and her accountant that she's very nervous about making financial decisions and would like them to teach her what they are doing and why. They can keep the powers of attorney that they have in case she is out of the country or in the event of an emergency, but while she's able she will participate in each decision. Despite her fear that he'd think she was asking for too much, she has asked her boyfriend to come to any financial meetings with her so that he can understand what's going on in her life. To this day her brain gets fuzzy when money conversations go on for any length of time.

Sarah still occasionally lends money, but now she expects to get it back . . . and so far, so good. Now that people know that's what is expected of them, things have gone pretty smoothly, with only a missed payment every now and then. And, even though it makes her stomach queasy to call her debtors, she does. She loves her family and friends but she is willing to let them get upset if necessary.

What Sarah realized was that she would rather make her own conscious decisions and take the risk of being wrong than have other people choose for her and take the risk of not liking the choices made for her anyway. She was entitled to all the success and love that she had in her life, and she was finally becoming comfortable with that concept. She didn't need to apologize for it or be embarrassed about it. She had earned it. Anyway, the team of helpers that she had selected to advise her were there to do just that. In not making what she considered to be decisions, in passing things off, she had been making decisions anyway. She had finally come to the bittersweet realization that no matter how she cut it she had been making choices all the time. As we all have done at one time or another, she had been choosing by not choosing. She deserved to choose openly and clearly *because it was her life that she was choosing for.*

Is Your Father Stuck in Your Throat?

He's a surgeon. She's a physical therapist. They grew up in Queens in middle-class families. He graduated from college and went on to medical school. While he was in medical school and she was working at the hospital they met, became sweethearts, and fell in love.

He completed his internship and residency, and she completed her training program. They supported each other emotionally and financially so that they could work toward their goals. He's 33, she's 32. They're married, live in Manhattan, and are expecting their first child.

I met Emily and Rob four years ago just after they had gotten married. He was sharing space with another doctor, getting referrals and building his practice by taking midnight calls to hospital emergency rooms. Emily was in practice as a physical therapist, specializing in care for the elderly. They are two of the nicest people I have ever met: warm, upbeat, hardworking.

They had been referred to me by an associate of Emily's, and when we met at my office they explained that they were on a fact-finding mission, interviewing me only to determine if they wanted to go ahead with a formal financial plan for themselves. People in their families and some friends had said that there was no need to speak to anyone about planning until they had substantial money to invest. As a matter of fact, Emily's uncle had pressed them into calling his expert accountant, the guy he'd been using for the last twenty-five years, to prove that they were too young and not successful enough to have an adviser. Uncle Lou had said, "You don't need to talk to somebody until you have something to talk about." And, in fact, the accountant had agreed with Uncle Lou. But they thought that they should still find out for themselves and were willing to hear what I had to say.

They were also sorry to inform me that they had no current investments or large cash balances in any bank accounts. No problem. Most people don't have investments when they start out, unless they inherit it or have trust funds. Most people don't have trust funds ever anyway, and if they do inherit money, it's often later on in life. So it's good to plan ahead. Think of it like this: You are going to build a dream house. The best way to have the house that you've always wanted is to picture what you want and then work with an architect to design it to your specifications. The first thing you need is to build a strong foundation. The stability of the house will be based on that. Planning makes all the difference!

That first time Emily and Rob and I spent about one hour together. They explained to me that since they had put themselves through college and graduate school, they each had student loans outstanding. The cost of education was high and they owed a lot of money on their loans. They also had paid for a big wedding just months earlier, and while they'd gotten gifts, they'd still spent more than they'd received. Now they were interested in developing a game plan to support their new life together, their growing practices, and to create a structure within which they could comfortably operate. They loved the concept of creating blueprints like an architect does.

Rob said that for the very first time he was feeling really grown up. Although they were still living in a one-bedroom apartment that was comfortable and affordable, they were hoping to move to a larger place soon, maybe even to buy a home. They wanted to figure out what they were looking at on a time line and create realistic goals, but they felt anxious about putting things in order. Everything seemed way beyond their reach. Neither of them had ever thought about long-range planning before, and it made them nervous.

By the time they left we had established that this was the best time to start planning and investing. If possible, planning should be done from the beginning—whether it's the beginning of a marriage, a career, a family, or a new life. It's a big help to focus on all the goals you have and figure out what it will take to get the things you don't have now but want to have in the future. In the beginning, you have the opportunity to work from a blank page and create the blueprints of a plan that you can follow instead of guessing your way through, like taking a trip without a map. Once a plan is created and in place, you have a map to guide you to make sure you have a safe journey. It's a lot easier to get somewhere if you are clear about your destination and the choices of roads to take to get there.

Oh yes, and there was that big question, never an easy one to answer: "Who do they think they are?" It was hard to break away from the way that things had been done in their families, and this was certainly different from the way things had been done. They were behaving in a way that was different from the way their parents, aunts, uncles, or cousins had behaved. For example, their parents had accumulated whatever they had by taking things day to day. They had never felt important enough to work with professionals to plan. Actually, their parents thought that only "big shots" plan. Rob's and Emily's families operated with the same philosophies. So if they chose a different course of action, were they acting like big shots? This was a tough one for them. The fact that they'd gone on in their education to become professionals didn't make them different from the kids they were when they grew up in Queens—did it? It was hard to break family patterns.

Big shots?

Change, regardless of whether it is for the better or not, makes people uncomfortable. When money comes into play, so do all kinds of deep feelings. One that I notice comes up a lot for men is: "Will I be as successful as my father; will I be able to follow in his path?" Another very powerful feeling that often stays unspoken on the tongues of men is "My father worked his entire life and never earned anything like this in income. I don't want him to feel bad and I don't want people to think I'm asking for too much." Rob expressed almost this identical thought to me: "My father never earned anything near what I do already. I wonder what he'll think; he'll probably tell me that I'm acting like a fancy man."

For Emily, the issue was a little different. She had never been taught anything about money while she was growing up. There was little if any discussion in her house about planning for the future. Her mother and father only "managed" to get by, even though both worked. Her mother kept telling her that being married to a doctor could be difficult, that in the beginning years all the money would be spent on building his practice, especially now, with the changes in insurance coverage. It could turn out that even with all the years invested in schooling, they'd end up with much less than they had planned for. Emily felt anxious about the future because of all the "be carefuls" that her mom was giving her.

What can we reasonably expect to do? Should we be very conservative in our lifestyle, or can we start working toward making our dreams come true now? What are we entitled to? These were Emily's concerns.

When you've never been taught, and you don't know anything other than the way you've lived and your parents have lived before you, planning for the future can be scary, even if the life ahead of you is one of success and prosperity. Graduating from college, any college, for any profession, does not automatically provide a graduate with financial expertise or sophistication. Ask anyone who's been there. Even MBAs don't know how to plan unless they specialize in personal financial theory. I know, because I have some of these bright men and women as clients. Ask my brother Steve, who's a doctor.

At every turn, each "little shot" you take along the road is a step toward becoming a "big shot," and each one of us deserves to have the biggest possible shot in life.

Rob likes to see things in black and white, and Emily is able to see the big picture and support the decisions that need to be made. They are a good team.

Rob wanted to start creating a plan right away and Emily agreed that that was the way to go. Both saw the value in using planning as a tool to reach their goals, so we set up a second meeting for one month later. That gave them time to gather the information we needed to start their plan and to focus on where they were spending their money. Each of them had school loans to pay off, but now Rob began to keep records of how he spent the rest of his money, and so did Emily. They got copies of their prior years' tax returns. They found out from their accountant what their projected tax liability was for the coming year, and retrieved an insurance policy from the back of the drawer. He had an individual retirement plan that he had started during his internship, and they reviewed that. She had some stock that she had been given as a graduation present. They gathered any and all information that they had about money. They wrote down everything for our next meeting.

At our next meeting we started to create a plan. It encompassed investing, education, retirement, estate planning (wills, life insurance, trusts), and risk management—that means any and all insurance protection, from health and disability to liability and homeowner's. We put together a time line. We created priorities. The most important things to Emily and Rob were saving for a new home, reducing their taxes, and long-term retirement planning. We talked about saving to buy a co-op and figured out that they could afford to save about $1,200 a month. They started pension plans, and each chose to participate in a **profit-sharing plan.** That way they could put away up to 15 percent of their earnings, get a tax deduction, and watch their money grow in a tax-deferred account until they retired. Contributions to profit-sharing plans are not mandatory, and they liked the flexibility this gave them. With all the talk about the possibility of there being no Social Security benefits sometime in the future, creating a retirement strategy made them feel more secure. In any case, even in the best of circumstances Social Security was never meant to provide all of anyone's retirement income. We agreed that they would send a monthly contribution to me for investment in the profit-sharing plan rather than coming up with one lump sum at every year-end. This would create a more balanced cash flow and decreased anxiety. They would talk to their accountant and figure out approximately what would be needed.

We worked on an asset allocation strategy so that their investments would reflect their attitudes and long-term goals. **Asset allocation** means dividing up the pie. It's deciding what percentage of money you are going to put into bonds, stocks that are conservative and stocks that are aggressive, international investments, and cash or cash equivalents if appropriate. We would discuss the available options at our next meeting.

Emily and Rob agreed that they wanted to purchase common stock and zero coupon bonds. They would accumulate the money that they contributed in a money market fund and then choose stocks that they had a particular interest in and buy shares. They would set up dividend reinvestment programs so that as they collected dividends more shares would be bought in the same company. They would also buy zero coupon bonds to represent the fixed-income or bond portion of the portfolio. Because they wanted to invest a small percentage of their retirement portfolio in international investments, they chose a mutual fund that specializes in global investing. This professionally managed portfolio gave them diversification with a small dollar investment. No money was kept in cash or short-term instruments because all these assets were to be invested for retirement.

I suggested they make an appointment to speak with an insurance specialist, and then we talked about the fact that using a plan takes time. The plan itself evolves and changes over time as life changes. Even the very first steps of a plan can take a year or more to put into place.

By our next meeting a month later the cornerstones of their plan were starting to be put in place. We talked about their meeting with the insurance specialist. Rob and Emily had both decided to buy life insurance as well as disability insurance. They had opened their profit-sharing plans and put a three-month emergency fund into a money market account. Now Rob was talking about expanding his practice, maybe buying a practice he had heard was becoming available from a retiring doctor.

We met again six months later to determine how much had been accomplished and where to go from there.

Now, more than two years later, Emily and Rob had saved almost the amount they needed as a down payment on a cooperative apartment. They were considering what price co-op they could afford. Rob was thinking of taking out a business loan to pay down their student loans: the interest on business loans is a tax deduction; the interest on student loans is not. Should they lease a car or continue to use taxis and rent cars? They talked about having a child soon.

Around the same time, another medical practice became available. Rob went to the bank and was able to increase his business loan. The doctor he bought the practice from was willing to take part of the purchase price as a down payment and the balance over the next five years. Rob consulted with his accountant, who reviewed the potential of the business and gave him the go-ahead. It looked like a good opportunity. Rob hired an attorney to assist in the negotiations, but handled the majority of the talks himself.

Emily's practice was growing too. She rented space so that she could see patients during regular office hours as well as make home visits.

They were starting to see their dreams come true. The more you see, the more you believe. This couple was really starting to believe in the value of having a plan.

Rob said that he was starting to become optimistic. He noticed that having a plan enabled him to measure their progress. Emily said that understanding how to do all these financial things was becoming easier. She had learned to read the various monthly and quarterly financial statements and knew what kinds of questions to ask the accountant. She was becoming more secure. Both said that they now realized how much their pasts had influenced the way they looked at their adult life choices when it came to money. Learning to deal with money in a structured way was like learning to speak a foreign language: the more they did it, the more comfortable they became. Even Uncle Lou was starting to notice that their plan was working and he gave Rob a pat on the back.

Rob and Emily bought an apartment three and a half years after the start of their plan. Emily handled getting all the information about a mortgage, calling the banks and finding out the rates. Together they learned the difference between fixed and variable rates and decided that based on their personalities, they would rather lock in at one rate for the life of the mortgage than take their chances on a rate that adjusted every year, even though the initial rate on the variable was lower. They took a fifteen-year fixed mortgage, agreeing that they preferred to pay higher monthly costs now and to have no mortgage to pay after the fifteen years were up. Finally, they had to figure out how much they needed to save in order to appropriately furnish the apartment.

Soon Emily became pregnant; Rob decided he wanted to spend more time with his wife, start enjoying the things they already had.

We met to figure out child care costs, and to plan their meeting with a lawyer to create a will and set up trusts for the new baby. Emily asked if they needed any more life insurance.

Rob was nervous about having enough money to provide his future daughter or son the best possible education. "I want my child to have a good education. You know, raising a child costs a lot of money. First there is a baby nurse, then nursery school, then lessons, and I just don't know how we'll be able to save all this."

I saw that he was genuinely upset. "Open your mouth," I said. "I think your father must be inside your mouth; that can't be you in there. I think your father has climbed right into your throat, or maybe that's Uncle Lou." He laughed; his energy shifted. "You're right. That's not even what I think; that's what my father would say."

Did you ever notice that when you speak about things that are important sometimes your parents' words jump right out? It has happened to almost everyone I know at one time or other. We take on our parents' beliefs without even being aware of it—it happens with money, with raising children . . . with almost every significant area of life. There is no escaping it, but hopefully we can recognize what is happening, and adjust our words and thoughts accordingly, if we choose to.

"Me too," said Emily. "Sometimes I just hear my mother speaking right out of my throat."

Rob continued: "When we first started to work together, I had a hard time accepting that I could plan and have things work out, that everything that I had dreamed about could be mine. I really didn't feel adept enough to handle things. I would just do something because you believed that we could make this work, and Emily and I believed in you. Now, even though my father climbs out of my throat from time to time, my own beliefs get stronger and I am becoming comfortable giving up my old ways of thinking."

Step by step, we started to figure out the cost of their child's schooling and how much they would have to save to make sure it was available. First they had to arrive at the cost of college in today's dollars. Emily asked, "Are you talking about Harvard or the state university?" Rob said, "Let's plan on Harvard." I said, "Are we talking about one lump sum, or saving over a period of time, and, if so, how long, what rate of inflation should we assume, and what rate of return?" They laughed. "Here we go again."

Later, Emily told me, "It gets better every day. I'm having fun with the planning process; it's structured, it gives me something to measure our progress with, and I can feel a sense of comfort that's beginning to develop out of working this way. The other day we went shopping for a layette and bought what we liked and wanted because we knew we'd earned it and we are able to give it to our baby, plus we feel safe in the knowledge that what we're doing fits within our plan. Working with a plan gives me peace of mind."

Rob was still nervous. He said, "When can we meet again so that we can go over the projections for education planning? I think my father wants to speak again!"

I told him, "The baby is due in three months, and we'll meet again before that. We will meet many more times after that, if my guess is right. That's the deal . . . the way life is. That's the journey we're on. There's always something new, something to plan for, to move toward or away from. There's always what's next and how to get there. Bring your father along for the ride—just don't let him steer."

Facts We Learned:

ENTITLEMENT

Adjustable rate mortgages will change rate periodically, going up or down depending on current market conditions.

You may use your home as collateral to secure additional financing. This is known as a home equity loan.

A power of attorney is used to allow another individual to sign documents or make decisions in your absence.

Financial planning consists of Investment, Education, Retirement, Risk Management, and Estate Planning.

Lessons We Learned:

ENTITLEMENT

Listen to the voices that whisper to you and tell you what you deserve . . . whose are they?

Be prepared to reject the ideas that are not really true for you.

Be clear about what *you* really think you are entitled to have in your life.

Intention is crucial to getting the desired results.

In the end you are your own judge and jury.

III.

RESPONSIBILITY

RESPONSIBILITY

1. Responsibility means _____.

2. When I am responsible I feel _____.

3. I am _____ responsible toward others than I am to myself.

4. Being responsible with money means _____.

5. The ways in which I am responsible are _____.

6. I feel _____ about borrowing money.

7. I feel _____ about lending money.

8. I am _____ about my future with money.

Responsibility

My friend, in the end,
no matter what you do . . .
You'll find that most of your life
Is up to you.

Grown Up?

When are you grown up? When does one grow up? Better yet, what is "grown up"?

Remember when you were a child, when you weren't allowed to do grown-up things? Did you know then that dentists and doctors cost money? Did the words "health insurance" have any real meaning in your vocabulary? Did you have a concept of rent or mortgage payment, credit, life insurance, or inflation? Me neither. The same for most people I know. Remember the feeling you had the first time you looked at your paycheck and saw what was left after Social Security and other taxes had been deducted? How could that be?

My friend Dottie has a younger brother, Barry, who is 22 years old. He works as a waiter at night, and is trying to break into stand-up comedy. One day he woke up with one of his legs swollen twice the size of the other. He had never been sick before and didn't know whom to call, so he took himself over to the emergency room of the local hospital, where he assumed that they would take care of him. He had no health insurance. Health insurance, after all, is seldom a focal point for young people like Barry. They know they aren't going to get sick. On a deeper level, health insurance is a responsibility that's been taken care of by parents; *it's a grown-up thing*. When they are no longer covered by parents, they don't think about it. Our boy was no different from most.

He also didn't know that there was a law that protected him: COBRA (the Consolidated Omnibus Reconciliation Act of 1986), the same act that allows people to maintain health insurance after loss of a job or spouse for eighteen months. It forbids a hospital to refuse treatment to a patient who has been admitted simply because the patient can't pay for it. Barry couldn't pay, but he was lucky because the hospital did admit him for treatment.

It was very upsetting for Barry to deal with social workers and people from the business office of the hospital. He felt lousy and vulnerable. His leg was killing him. They still needed to talk to him about how he was going to pay the bill. He was over 21 and he was responsible. But worrying about health insurance was for grown-ups, and until this moment he had not considered himself a grown-up; not like his mother and father and older sister Dottie were grown up.

Not having health insurance was a mess. It was true that the hospital had to take him in, but not all doctors accept patients who aren't covered by private insurance or HMOs. He would rather have had a specific doctor whom a friend had told him about, but she was affiliated with an HMO and Barry was not. As it happened, the doctor who took care of him was very nice, and Barry's parents offered to pay for her services. Neither Barry's sister nor his parents could afford to pay for his entire hospital bill, but his parents did make the first few payments toward the new health plan they insisted he get.

Then the fun part began. These days health insurance is a complicated matter, even for grown-ups. Depending on your ability to pay, your medical history, and general insurability, you may have to make different decisions from the ones you thought you would. In that sense, for Barry, this was a very interesting time. He was starting to think that he might just be growing up and the thought did not please him all that much. This thought does upset some people. Barry found out that as an individual not covered by a company, he was quite limited in his options. Programs offered through large corporations to their employees were unavailable to single subscribers. In the process of learning what was available to him, Barry discovered that the condition he was being treated for would not be covered by any new health insurance plan for at least one year because it was considered a preexisting condition. Ouch!

The least expensive and most efficient way for Barry to deal with health insurance was to buy a plan with a large deductible. He would pay his premium monthly, and if he got sick he would have to pay the first $3,000 out of pocket; that $3,000 would not be reimbursed. After that, the insurance company would pay for everything on a split of 80-20—in other words, his insurer would pay 80 percent and Barry would pay 20 percent of any outstanding medical bills related to his illness. He did have some savings. The hospital costs would be covered 100 percent. Basically, Barry was a healthy guy with limited cash flow. He was betting that the only medical costs he would face would be for occasional office visits to the doctor, and that the main purpose of his insurance was to be covered for a catastrophe like the one he was experiencing now.

The good news was that it turned out Barry had developed an allergic reaction to an insect bite—that the swelling in his leg had not been the result of illness. He was discharged after only two days of hospitalization. Two days later he signed up for an insurance plan. Nice scare. Welcome to the adult world!

When my son Jonathan was 18 years old, he left New York to travel around the world and find himself. He was a big shot in those days. He put a knapsack on his back and didn't look back. The one thing that he did take with him was an American Express card. I guess those commercials work; I told him, no matter what, don't leave home without it. Make sure that you have some protection for emergencies. Other than that, he was on his own.

Somewhere about a year into his adventure he met Inger. She had also decided to see the world after graduating from high school and had left her home in Saskatchewan, Canada, to do it. They met on a boat traveling from Greece to Israel and have been together ever since. Isn't that incredibly romantic? I think so.

The way they tell the story, they pooled all their monies and shared everything. They had a few articles of clothing that they carried with them as they went from place to place. They felt very grown up and self-sufficient. They paid their own way and took care of their own needs. They took jobs as construction workers, as waiters, as bicycle messengers, and as theater ticket clerks. Before returning home, they went as far as Thailand and India.

It was in India that the juicy part of this story begins. They called home to ask me if they could make some purchases with my American Express card. They had a great idea about how to make money and they wanted to know if they could pay me back when they got home. Sure, no problem!

So, they visited a local merchant and bought inexpensive jewelry and art—many pairs of earrings and bracelets as well as prints. It was their intention to bring back these items and resell them to friends or local stores. Their entire investment was to be $1,500 American. They would have everything sold by the time the bill came from American Express and would use the proceeds to repay me. You can see where this story is heading, right?

Well, they did get home safe and sound. They weren't feeling all that well from living on a diet of sticky rice, but they were home and happy to be back, armed with their purchases and ready to go into business. Then the bill from American Express showed up. I remember it well: I opened the bill and lost my breath. The bill for the local Indian merchant was $7,500. What had happened? Had they lost their minds? But Jonathan and Inger couldn't believe the bill either. They were positive they had spent nowhere near that amount of money. With the three of us standing in my kitchen I called American Express customer service and had the bill frozen. Jon and Inger looked like they were going to faint. I was sure that things would get resolved; there was clearly a mistake.

About a month later we got a letter explaining that the merchant who sold the goods said that the bill was correct—I owed the money. If, however, Jonathan could produce his copy of the bill, then they would reopen the case. Jonathan says that the bill was lost when his knapsack fell into the Ganges River. No evidence, no case.

Couldn't something be done? Jonathan and Inger were growing older and wiser by the day. We were becoming experts on credit card use. I requested a copy of the bill that Jonathan had signed. It had his signature all right; it looked like our man in India had played with the receipt. The bill was in rupees, and he had clearly added some zeros at the end. When we enlarged it on the copier machine you could clearly see that. There was our evidence. Back to American Express. They were very gracious and asked if Jonathan would like to file a fraud claim. He could have one signed by his witness—Inger— as well, and that should do it. They kept the charge off my bill until things were cleared up. Any day now.

Jonathan was getting annoyed and frustrated. "Why can't they just see that we have proof? Besides, Inger is a witness. Losing my receipt was an accident; can't they see that?" Inger too was getting scared. "What if they don't believe us? What if we have to pay the whole amount?" Oh yes, and American Express also wanted us to know that their cards are not to be used to purchase items intended for resale. Their client agreement strictly forbids that.

It took about a year for this mess to be handled. We learned that a consumer is not protected for customer fraud outside the United States. We learned that American Express had sent a representative in India to talk to the vendor, and in the end all we had to pay was what we had always known was the correct amount. Yes, ultimately they were very gracious.

We each had added a few gray hairs. Yes, all of us. Especially for Jonathan and Inger, this had been a rite of passage.

Remember feeling you had earned a notch in your belt after handling something that you had never dreamed you could handle? Those first times when you are blindsided and somehow keep on your feet are the ones that stay with you forever.

My Grandmother the Layaway Queen, or The Games People Play

My paternal grandmother may have been the very first layaway queen of Brooklyn. In case you've never heard of it, layaway was one of the original forms of shopping on credit. You'd go to the store and pick out what you liked, then leave a deposit at the store so that the owner would hold it for you until you had paid the entire amount. Sometimes people came back week after week, applying small amounts toward the total purchase price until they'd paid in full and could finally take their prize purchases with them.

My father's mother, Gussie, loved to buy fine things, and she often did. The only problem with this was that she and my grandfather had very little money. They lived in Brooklyn in a ghetto neighborhood called Brownsville, where many immigrants settled after coming from Russia. My grandfather worked in a sweatshop sewing men's suit pants and jackets, and Grandma stayed home and took care of the house. They were a very traditional couple. In those days operators (that's what my grandfather was) got paid by the number of garments that they sewed. The work was seasonal. More suits were bought in fall and winter than in spring and summer, and workers got paid only when they worked, so money had to be apportioned so that there would be some left when no work was available. They had four children and money was scarce. It was hard enough to make do from payday to payday, never mind buying wonderful things. For my grandmother, however, that was only a wrinkle, not an out-and-out obstacle. This was how she discovered layaway and, boy, was she good at it!

My earliest memories included going to my grandparents' home and seeing what we lovingly referred to as tchotchkes (known in other circles as knickknacks or bric-a-brac). They were of assorted designs, materials, and shapes; no one else I knew had items such as these in their homes. There were doilies of fine linen and porcelain cats and dogs. The living room was filled with crystal dishes and china. My grandmother had a fine eye and grand taste, and was also notorious for her strict rules about behavior in the living room. Nothing was to be touched without her permission, and in fact she never actually granted permission to touch anything—except for one ceramic dog that looked like a black-and-white cocker spaniel and one gray-and-white porcelain cat. (I still have that cat; she sits in my living room to this very day.) Almost every item in that living room had been bought at Fortunoff, a store known for its giftware and home furnishings, a store filled with things from all over the world that any homemaker would just love to have had; there were lamps and dishes, china and silver. When my grandmother took me there, it made me feel heady to look at all those wonderful, special things. In my memory it feels the same as the first time I visited a museum: a sense of grandeur filled the store. These were not things for ordinary people; they were magical, to be both coveted and respected. At least that's what I learned from the way that Grandma Gussie behaved there. When she walked among the rows of stemware and dishes, she stood a little taller. This was her domain.

My grandmother may well have been one of Fortunoff's earliest customers. Since those days, Max Fortunoff and his family have seen their business grow, with stores throughout New York City. But in the late 1940s and '50s they had one location—and it was within walking distance for my grandmother. Since walking was her only mode of transportation, this was key. Fortunoff offered no delivery service, so Grandma had to carry her purchases home or arrange for one of the kids in the neighborhood to be the delivery boy if the item was a big thing like a lamp or a curio cabinet. A lot of thinking and planning went into these purchases!

In our family the stories about Grandma Gussie and her shopping habits were repeated over and over. On her routine visits, she always found something that she just had to have. She would make sure that her selection met her criteria for craftsmanship as well as display. Then she would give it to the salesclerk to hold for her, along with a layaway deposit. Each week she would visit her acquisition, ask to see it one more time, and after looking it over lovingly, examining it for flaws or any overlooked details, she would return it, giving the clerk a few more cents to hold toward the total purchase price. Each visit would bring her that much closer to having her new possession. Finally her precious new object would be fully paid for and she could take it home.

Once home, she would perform the next part of the ritual. She would unpack it, look it over once more, then repack it up in the third bedroom. The other two bedrooms in my grandparents' home were designated for sleeping, but the third bedroom was known as the storeroom. It had a mysterious quality about it, kind of like an old attic. It was my grandmother's version of a walk-in closet, before there was such a thing. In the storeroom, she would find a safe spot for her precious addition and leave it there until the time was appropriate to display it. Somehow she knew just when that was. I don't know for sure, but I guess that by then she had already selected another "must have" thing and was starting a new layaway cycle. In any case the tchotchke in question would remain in waiting in the storage room for at least one month and sometimes as many as three months, depending on the cost and significance of the item, and then, one day, it would appear. It would show up in the kitchen or living room or bedroom, wherever it rightfully belonged. No explanation, no discussion . . . it would just be there. It was time.

My grandfather, Papa Louie, would come home from work and sit down for dinner. Then, after his meal, he would go into the living room to listen to the radio or read the Jewish newspaper, or he might go into his bedroom to change into comfortable clothing. And he would see it. He would see the new must-have item that had just been unveiled.

"What's this, Gussie?"

"What are you talking about, Louie?"

"What do you mean what am I talking about—this new lamp here in the living room, Gussie."

"What new lamp, Louie?"

"Right here, Gussie, the green-and-gold one right in front of my face."

"That's not a new lamp; where have you been? Are you so tired that you can't see what goes on in this house every day? Don't tell me this is the first time that you noticed this lamp."

"Are you trying to make me crazy? This is a new lamp. I have never seen it before."

"How can that be? It's been in the house for more than two months now."

"We don't have enough money to buy things; we need the money for food and bills."

"I didn't take away from the family. Are you feeling like you are missing something? Besides which, that's not a new lamp."

And so it went. The game they played with each other went on just like that until the day my Papa Louie died. By then they had been married over forty years. Their house was filled with loads of things that had just shown up over the years.

Their story was always told with a laugh and a little bitterness—about how Grandma was always spending and poor Papa couldn't keep up with her. Everyone living in the house had played a part, even the children. They knew. But if all the children in the family knew what was going on, I can only assume Papa did too. So, if Papa had known how the game worked all along, why hadn't he tried to stop it?

Oh, my: they were both in the game! My Papa was not a stupid man; he was not formally educated, but he was smart. They say he was tired and he didn't have the energy to argue. They say that in any case there was no changing my determined grandmother if she wanted something. So he had been aware and he had chosen to know and say nothing. By saying nothing, by not being willing to make waves, he had become as responsible as my grandmother for each new tchotchke that had shown up in the house. *They had each played a part in the game. Otherwise there wouldn't have been a game.*

I'll bet you hear stories like this all the time. One spends and the other is a victim. No way! It takes two. Partners do this kind of thing all the time: they collude with each other, agree to not see and *willingly* play victim. Not just married couples, not just male and female couples—partners in all kinds of situations cut deals with each other.

Parents and children play like Papa and Grandma. So do business partners. Papa was not an innocent after all, and neither is anyone who is willing to participate in the layaway game.

Kirsten is a very bright and witty woman in her sixties, recently widowed. On my last visit to her home we were talking about how she was doing alone now that her husband wasn't making her financial decisions. She had been on her own for more than a year now.

Curtis had always made all the financial decisions while he was alive. Now Kirsten had turned to me and her attorney for guidance. Curtis had left instructions that at the time of his death all the money was to be placed in a trust for Kirsten's use. "Oh," she said, "now that he's gone I have you and other people to take care of my money for me, and I have what I need. There really isn't anything monetary that I want for. Well, thank God I was left comfortable, but I would have preferred that Curtis had left the money to me outright instead of in a trust. It's not so wonderful having to go ask another person for some extra money. Curtis said he'd set it up that way because I wasn't experienced with money, but I think he thought I'd spend it foolishly. We always had money, but Curtis and I didn't always agree on how to spend it, so I had to become creative to have what I wanted. It was our little game. You know what I'm talking about."

I didn't know. "What little games?" I asked.

"Well, when I used to go shopping, I would pay for 50 to 60 percent on my credit card and the rest in cash. All the storekeepers knew that I split the bill. That way Curtis would never know how much I spent. I loved to go shopping and I'm a good shopper, but Curtis and I didn't agree on how much was enough. By only giving him the bills for half on the credit card I saved him from getting all riled up. I didn't work, but I got the rest of the money from checks that I cashed for household money. A smart person can always find a way, and I consider myself a smart person. That's how I got around in our system. It didn't hurt anybody and it meant we didn't fight . . . once I understood how to handle him. In the beginning I was honest, and we fought. What's the point of that?!

"Well, maybe, now that I think about it, he must have known. He was an awfully sharp businessman and he must have guessed that I was spending all that cash on something. But if he did, he never let on. He would make jokes right in front of my kids about all the clothes I had in the closet with the tags still on, but he never said a word to me about kicking my shopping habit. He complimented me about the bargains I found wherever I went. My kids think he knew but just wasn't willing to fight with me, or to concede openly. We had found a way to handle the problem without discussing it. He didn't ask too many questions and I didn't offer any more explanations. Of course I would have preferred to have been honest with him, but you just couldn't be honest with Curtis about spending. It would have been nicer if I didn't have to sneak around; we lived like that for over thirty-five years. I'll bet that's why he didn't leave me in charge of my own money.

"I'm sure my children learned some funny lessons from the way we acted. After all, you know you can't live in a house and see your parents' behavior without picking up some of it yourself."

I think the lady may have had a point!

Then there was Micki and Joshua. For years, every time I saw Micki, she told me how Joshua treated her like a princess. What she really loved about this man was that he was so thoughtful and generous. He was always buying her presents and taking her to wonderful restaurants. The only thing was, they never saved any money, and she yearned to buy her own home someday. When I asked how much they were making, Micki said that she really didn't know, that Josh was in charge of the finances and that the money he made as a commissioned salesperson varied from month to month. Because she was often away on business, he was in charge of handling their money, including paying the bills. "When I ask him about our money situation, he tells me not to worry, so I don't," she told me. "I don't want him to think I don't trust him. It would upset the quality of our relationship."

The last time I saw Micki she was looking miserable. She had received a call from one of her credit card issuers telling her that she was past due on her bill. She'd had no idea. Josh had told her that things were fine and she'd believed him. Now, as she spoke with the representative, she found out that not only was she past due but the amount of money she owed on her credit card was, as she put it, "huge." She and Josh had been using all the credit cards to the max and been paying only the minimum payments. He'd been using MasterCard to pay Visa. They were in serious financial trouble.

"The worst part is that I know I've played a big part in all of this. I wanted to think that I had the best, the sweetest guy in the whole world to be married to. So I let him keep charging the gifts he bought me, knowing deep down that we couldn't afford all those things. By not questioning him, I allowed the charade to continue. Frankly, I wonder whether I ever would have said anything if the lady from the credit card company hadn't called. Now we fight all the time. He's angry with me for being so surprised about the situation. Maybe he's right. I suppose I just didn't want to know the truth."

I know the feeling. You remember I told you I had been in a financially incompatible marriage. When I was married I had an image of what marriage was supposed to be. I wanted to have it the way I thought it was supposed to be, at all costs. So, when I was eight months pregnant and found out that my husband had spent all the money we had in the bank on a "business venture" without talking to me first, I decided not to tell anyone. I knew I could leave him, but that didn't feel like a choice to me. I pretended that everything was all right to the rest of the world. I pretended it was all right with me. The rules were simple: Don't ask questions that you don't want the answers to. I was not prepared to change anything, so I stopped asking questions. If you don't ask, you don't have to deal with the issues raised. I kept hoping a miracle would come my way and I wouldn't have to confront what felt like an insurmountable problem.

Over the years after that, I knew we were often in serious financial difficulty, but I really didn't want to know just how bad it was. I felt helpless to change things. But the evidence kept creeping in all around me. There were unpaid bills, we owed money on credit cards, and we disagreed all the time about what we could afford. We had very different ways of operating with money.

I had to do something. There were too many things for me to make believe about and it was getting too hard to make believe at all. There was always a story, always an explanation, and I would hang on to them for dear life, and then I finally decided to do the unthinkable. It was really hard. I was afraid to change the status quo but I could no longer live making up stories to myself. I was unwilling to play the game anymore. *I was no longer willing to make believe that things were manageable.* It had taken years before I made the decision to change the rules of the game, before I threatened to leave the marriage . . . to stop being a victim. When I finally did, my husband was very shocked. He didn't deny that we were drowning, he just resented that I was unwilling to overlook it anymore. I did change the rules of the game . . . no more make-believe, no more stories—and I don't regret it. But it was a very difficult time. I had to assume personal responsibility for everything that had happened. I much preferred thinking of myself as the victim. Don't we all?

Collusion is common. It may even appear to be just like "little games." We tell ourselves that a little white lie is no big deal, that life is easier. After all, who's really getting hurt? But the truth is people do get hurt. Sometimes making believe causes very serious damage. It takes two willing and active participants to form a collusion, two people who don't want to rock the boat, to change their lifestyle, or to be seen in a different light. Curtis knew about Kirsten and Micki knew about Joshua. No innocents here. I think that Papa knew what Grandma was up to and didn't want to fight; maybe he liked the things that she bought and felt guilty that he couldn't give her more, so he just kept silent. Whatever the reasons, he made the choice to live his entire life with my grandmother and never change. They were in the game together.

Now, if you are involved in some similar type of financial collusion *you do* have the option to change. If you decide that you want to change your relationship with your partner, to stop the games that you play with each other, it requires that you be willing to deal with your fear of change. What in fact are you afraid of? What can happen to the relationship if you begin to be honest? What are the questions you have been afraid to ask? In order for things to change—for the games to stop—you need to *begin to ask the questions you don't want the answers to! In order to have your life be different, the old games need to stop now!*

Smoke and Mirrors

You've all heard the expression "using smoke and mirrors." It describes an attempt to distort reality by changing the perception of things without really changing anything at all. The smoke is used to cloud the space and the mirrors create the image of making things larger. It's a great illusion.

Many people use the same kind of imagery to allude to the reality of their finances. You must know some of them. Maybe you're one yourself.

When the world that you're living in is full of smoke and mirrors you can separate things out and put them into little packages. That way you can look at parts of the whole without ever having to focus on the entire package. You create financial illusion. Actually, if you're good at creating smoke and mirrors you will probably fool even yourself about what's going on in your financial life. You act as though life is just fine. You may have some money in the bank or may even have investments in stocks, bonds, and mutual funds. Maybe you even own your house or apartment. You have a good job, take vacations from time to time, and you're handling things. *You probably also owe a lot of money.* You have a mortgage, a car loan or lease, and owe lots of money to the credit card company. You may have consolidated your debts to a wonderful low-rate card and are now paying a *minimum* every month that is manageable. You feel in control most of the time, except for once or twice a month when you sit down to pay your bills.

The amount of money you owe is increasing because the interest you're paying is eating away at every payment. Very little or none of the principal you owe is being paid off; and not only that, the rate of interest you are paying to the credit card company is higher than the return you're getting on your investments. It feels good to have some money in the bank. But whose money is actually in the bank or invested in the mutual funds you have bought? It's like having a pair of pants with two pockets. You're filling up one pocket with all kinds of goodies while there is a hole in the other pocket that everything is falling out of. Both pockets belong to the same pair of pants, *your* pants. When you live in the world of smoke and mirrors you operate as though each pocket is separate. When all is said and done and you take everything out and lay it on the table, you have the net sum of everything. If you've been living like this, maybe it's time for you to look around at the illusion surrounding you.

Matt and Lynda have been going together for two years and recently decided to get married. They're both college graduates. He's an accountant (but don't think because he handles numbers day in and day out, he's got it all together). She's a teacher. They live together now and are planning to have a wedding next fall. Their parents are helping to pay for the wedding, but they'll still have to come up with some money toward the bill. (Weddings are very expensive these days, and Lynda has two other sisters who would like to have big weddings one day.) Matt's father is semiretired and helps pay tuition for a son who is still in school.

Matt and Lynda each owe about $25,000 to the banks on their student loans, which need to be paid off over the next ten years, starting immediately, at the very reasonable rate of 7 percent. Somehow they never thought the day would come when they would have to start paying back the money. Lynda said that when the "college loan coupon book" showed up at her house at first she couldn't figure out what it was for. Then the light went on and it took her breath away for a minute. The time when she would have to start making payments on her student loan had seemed so far in the future. Now she was holding the book; the time had come. In fact, the $25,000 that she had borrowed to finance her education will end up costing her somewhere around $35,000 to $40,000 by the time she's done with interest. Thinking about owing that much money makes her nervous, so she and Matt prefer to think of it as

$250 a month (not small, but much smaller than $25,000) for what feels like forever.

Matt just cashed in the **savings bonds** he had gotten as birthday and graduation gifts over the years to pay for a $5,000 engagement ring. It's a beautiful diamond, a solitaire setting, and as he said, Lynda deserves it and it makes him feel good to be able to give it to her. The money is gone, and the ring is on Lynda's hand, and Matt will owe the government taxes on all the money his bonds earned over the years while interest was accumulating. The reason he owes taxes now is that EE savings bonds are issued by the U.S. government and we buy them at a discount to their face value. The face value is what they will be worth someday in the future at the time of a pre-determined maturity. We get no interest or dividend payments made to us while we own them. The government does not charge any tax until the bonds are cashed in. When they are cashed in we get back the original money invested and any interest due us. At that time we owe taxes on the difference between the original amount that was paid and the value at the time of redemption. The amount of taxes that are paid is based on each person's current tax bracket at the time of redemption. Rates paid on the bonds have fluctuated over the years, but when you buy them you will be told in advance just how long they will take to mature.

When I was a kid we used to spend $18.75 and give someone a bond that said $25 face value. Now EE bonds are issued for higher amounts. They take years to double. You pay $25 for $50 in the future. We used them for births, graduations, weddings, and religious confirmations of all denominations. If I was invited to a Bar Mitzvah, that's what my parents had me give as a gift. I always thought it was a great idea and I still do. When my boys decided to go traveling they cashed in the EE bonds they had gotten when they were born and at other special occasions during their lives. It was nice to have that money saved. I'll bet many an engagement ring, college tuition, and backpacking trip was paid for thanks to EE bonds.

Since Matt's in a top tax bracket now because he's still single and earning a nice salary ($55,000 a year), he's gonna have a hefty tax bite. Had he known that he was going to cash in these bonds, he probably would have been better off doing it when he was a student and had no other income. Lower income usually means a lower tax bracket. Most people don't worry about their tax brackets when they're students—they pay no taxes. So now: he got the money, he spent the money, he bought the ring, she's wearing the ring, and he's about to pay the tax bill.

Actually they both will, since they've decided to pool all their monies. Now they have to figure out where they're going to get the money to pay the taxes. But the ring is absolutely beautiful—I saw it.

Both Matt and Lynda grew up in rental apartments and they want to have a home of their own. Their goal is to buy a house in five years and they want to know how much to start putting away every month so that they can reach their objective. In addition to their student loans, they also owe money to two credit card companies, and to the car loan company. The car is brand-new so they have more than four years left to pay on that. They keep paying minimum charges to Visa and MasterCard each month and are trying not to add any more charges, but they say that sometimes they just don't have any alternative but to use them, especially around holiday season. (What did we all do before credit cards?) They have been able to accumulate $3,000 in savings at their bank, and that makes them very happy. At least they feel it's a start. Or is it?

We have a problem here! The bank is paying 3.2 percent interest. The friendly credit card company has given them a consolidated loan for their $5,000 of debt at a rate of 6.9 percent, and the interest is accruing daily. "Accruing" is an accounting word that means building up or accumulating. Either the entire amount of money owed has to be paid off completely, right away, or interest charges start getting added to their bill for the original money borrowed, and interest on the interest. And then, on top of that, if they use the credit card to make any new purchases, there is often no grace period because there already is an outstanding balance. If you read a credit card agreement it tells you that right on the piece of paper. You got it: the meter that measures interest due keeps running all the time. A grace period is a period of time when you don't have to pay for the items you've charged and no interest is accruing. That usually happens when you are carrying no balance. You may be beginning to notice that this way of handling finances can become expensive, confusing, and downright difficult.

Matt and Lynda could pay down a good chunk of the credit card debt, but they love having savings in the bank and they don't want to stop putting money away for the dream house that they've planned to buy five years down the road. Welcome to the world of smoke and mirrors. The 3.2 percent that they are receiving on their savings is fully taxable. So, depending on their tax bracket, they may only be keeping somewhere around 2 percent. The money that they are paying the credit card company is not tax deductible at all. If I'm counting right, after all is said and done they are out of pocket about 5 percent on their money, all because they want to *think* that they have savings. Here's how I figure it: You make two, you spend seven—it costs you five.

$3000 x 2% = $60 earned
$3000 x 7% = *$210 spent*
net 5% = $150 difference out of pocket

It's like that pair of pants with the pocket that has a hole in it. If Matt and Lynda paid off the credit card debt, they would be saving the 7 percent charge. However, in order to do that they would have to give up the illusion of having real savings. The reason I say "illusion" is that they have really borrowed money from the credit card company and put it in the bank. Call me crazy, but I think that's a high price to pay for wanting to make believe you have security. As a matter of fact, if they were to use their money to pay off the debt on their credit cards, they would be that much closer to really saving.

Just in case you're thinking that only unsophisticated people fall into thinking this way, you're wrong. All kinds of people do, even those who have the ability to pay off their bills, because they don't want to deplete their "savings." They like the concept of having money in the bank. In the end, of course, they would be better off paying off the bills and using the credit card or credit lines only if an emergency arose and they needed to use credit as an alternative. In the meantime, they would have stopped paying interest charges. Then they could really start saving.

The numbers don't lie. It's up to you to decide what price you are willing to pay for the illusion you want to create. *Sometimes we just don't want to know the truth about how things work.* It's hard to get where you're going if you don't even want to accept where you're starting from.

I suggested that Matt and Lynda take what they had considered their savings and pay down their credit card debt. Matt wasn't happy about this plan. He even suggested that it would slow up their future by depleting their savings, and that it would take that much longer to get their house. Accountant or not, he could not see the logic of our discussion. He really believed that the money in the bank was theirs and was the beginning of a nest egg, and he didn't want to look at the facts. Well, actually, he *was* willing to look at the *information;* he was just unwilling to see the *truth.* The facts upset him, and he didn't want to get upset. Once he was able to really look at the numbers, they made sense to him, but he wasn't happy. He had liked the way things looked before. Before, he had money in the bank, and that made him feel good. But once he saw that he and Lynda were only rearranging things and that there was a way they could get to their goals faster, he agreed. He and Lynda made a decision to keep $500 in the bank as a security cushion and use the rest to pay down their credit card bills. This was a real beginning.

Don't be upset with yourself if this is how you or someone you care about lives. You need to have a sense of humor about it. My friend Annie was starting her acting career. She had accumulated $6,500 in savings. She also paid her Visa bills with the checks from her MasterCard credit line. She prided herself on the fact that she always paid more than her minimum and couldn't figure out why her bills were growing, even though she hadn't bought anything on credit in the last month. That's right—her minimum was less than the interest charges.

One day we talked about the world of smoke and mirrors. She got the idea right away. She actually laughed at the world of illusion that she had produced for herself. Blowing away the smoke, being willing to face facts, made a big difference to her. Annie used most of her savings to pay off her bills. Looking into the future, she knew that in case of emergency she could always call on her plastic pals, and she kept some savings in reserve to feel safe, just like Matt and Lynda. There's nothing wrong in holding something back this way if it increases your security level, as long as you are reasonable. (I say feelings are important fiscal components!) That was a year ago. Now, Annie has really begun to save. Earlier she had deposited *borrowed money* to her account and was going nowhere. Now she has a real savings account. Annie likes to say that she used to be the leading lady in "the world of smoke and mirrors."

In a perfect world, we would all save money with ease, handle our finances with no anxiety, and never have to worry about our financial circumstances. But those of us living in the real world have to live with being less than perfect ourselves.

Ghettohead

What's a ghettohead? Somebody who thinks she's never gonna get out of her situation and that life is never gonna be better than it is at this moment. Folks like this never move out of their own mental ghetto. They live only in the moment, never planning for a future. Feeling powerless to change their destiny, they settle for immediate gratification.

These are the people, living in their ghettohead mentality, who buy fancy cars, VCRs, take great vacations, and go on shopping sprees saying, "Why shouldn't I have it now? It won't make a difference in the long run." We understand it when we see it in the real ghetto, when people buy clothes and radios they can't afford while living in over-crowded apartments with no hope. They spend hard-earned money on lottery tickets, hoping that life will change for them someday, but not that *they* will change. But we miss the connection when we or our middle-class pals behave this way; we think we're different.

Sometimes ghettoheads look sad or confused, but most of the time they look just fine! They are living in the moment, after all, and the moment feels okay. It's only when you sit down to talk to them, really talk about what matters, that something seems funny. You begin to understand that they have little hope for the future. In fact, they really don't think about it. When thoughts of the future show up in their heads, they shake them out quickly because the future is too painful or too vague to think about. It's always all about *now.*

The 1980s was a time of conspicuous consumption and debt. We were younger, and some of us were less wise. Whether you are in your twenties, thirties, forties, fifties, or even older, life is different now for most of us than it was in the eighties. The world was different: unemployment was lower, salaries were higher, and businesses were expanding, not downsizing. Good times and hope for the future were in sight. Our financial expectations were different, based on what we personally experienced, heard on television, and read in print. Our perception of how things were and would continue to be changed in the eighties. We were able to find jobs coming out of school that we had never thought possible. We had credit cards, two homes, good cars. We were refinancing our homes and apartments. We were using that money to buy more of everything. Banks gave us credit to buy boats and to take vacations. Oh yes, I remember it well.

Now some of us find ourselves with less savings, poor planning, and minimal understanding of the complexities of living in the nineties. We find ourselves with bills and burdens, less energy, and less time to accomplish things. We played hard, we worked hard (and we still do). And a lot of us feel tired. We have young children, old parents, more responsibility, less energy. We feel as if we will never get to where we want to be financially. So we spend instead, get to feel good right now, and leave tomorrow to tomorrow. Sometimes it's not about how much money we have or how much we need. Sometimes it's about not seeing light at the end of the tunnel, or even making a plan to get out of the tunnel.

What to do? How can you get out of that ghettohead behavior?

What have you noticed about ghettoheads? They do the most damage to their finances when they are alone or with other ghettoheads. Most ghettoheads go shopping and spend money and buy things that are okay but not great. They are only temporarily satiated, soon dissatisfied again. They have no idea of how much they spend. They shop most often by credit card. They are impulse buyers. They love immediate gratification.

But truly, there is help. If you or someone you know is a ghettohead, don't despair. This is the time for change. Band together!

Steps for Curing the Financial Ghettohead:

1. Partner up with someone who will understand and support your desire to leave the financial ghetto.
2. Shop with a buddy . . . Make sure the buddy you shop

with does not have the same weakness you do when it comes to recreational shopping. Never shop alone unless it is an emergency.

3. Shop only in places where you can return things.
4. Talk to yourself (out loud if need be). Ask yourself these questions:

   > *Why am I doing this?*
   > *Do I really need this?*
   > *Will this help me and in what way?*
   > *How else can I handle this impulse?*

5. Do whatever you need to do to avoid going to that cash register or repeating that credit card number to someone over the phone.
6. Find alternatives to satisfy your needs.
7. Pay with cash.
8. Don't despair even if you ghetto-head again. Change takes time.

Of course, it's easier to pay with plastic. It doesn't feel like money. It wasn't made to feel like money. Those credit card people are no dopes. *Use cash.* An interesting concept! If you really want to experience paying with real money, *pay for every purchase with nothing larger than a $5 bill.* Use the ATM or cash a check at the bank and request that the teller give you only fives and singles. Now put away your credit cards for at least thirty days, and even your checkbook, and use this money to pay for all your purchases. You may notice an odd sensation as each bill leaves your palm, causing you to truly experience spending.

Beverly recently told me that when she first decided to get serious about her impulse spending, she knew she had to get rid of her credit cards. She would freeze them until further notice. So she put her credit cards in a plastic glass filled with water and then put the glass in the freezer. If she got the urge to use the card she would have to wait until it had thawed sufficiently. The amount of time it took for the ice to melt was enough for her to chill out and come to her senses.

Give the credit cards to someone else to hold if you can't trust yourself. Partner up with a friend or financial adviser.

Michelle got a settlement from an insurance company years ago after she had been in an accident. Since that time she's invested the money and has for the most part been very responsible about her spending. She credits her sensibleness to the fact that she knows she will have to call me to get money from her account if the bills are greater than her income. She doesn't like doing that! So far, the strategy is working and her investments have grown.

Buy a piggy bank and save at home, or open a savings account at the bank. If you do the piggy routine, make sure it doesn't have a hole in its belly where you can retrieve money easily. Get a plastic, see-through piggy so you can see it pile up. Put away the money you don't spend. You may be forgoing interest for a while, but you can see cash build. Some people need that. Deposit money to your bank account first when you have your money. *Don't wait to see what's left over . . . there will never be anything left over.* Do the saving first.

Some of the assistants in my office got together recently and decided that they were going to bag lunch and save the difference. They were going on a saving spree. The money that they saved would be deposited in a Christmas club at the local bank. This Christmas club pays interest on all deposits. Each woman has her own coupon book and has made a separate commitment to the group. The money gets deposited on payday. That's right, payday, before it can find another place for itself. They rotate who will be in charge of collection and going to the bank to make the deposits. There is a team spirit and they support each other in keeping their promises. They will tell you that you have to take the money right from the top; otherwise it just disappears.

Be willing to be different from who you were before; be willing to be different from some of the ghettoheads around you. It's a new way of living, so it will probably feel uncomfortable at first. *Appreciate yourself for every small step that you take.*

Save your credit card receipts and take a hard look at them to figure out where you have been spending. Stop stuffing them in pockets or losing them or throwing them out with the bag that you carried home from the store. Really look at those bills. Did you need the coat that's hanging at the back of the closet just because it was on sale? What about that new winter coat for your pet dog Sheba? Don't say that you spend your money on Visa and American Express. What are you using Visa and American Express for? Do you shop by catalog? That's another painless and powerful way to spend without having to leave your seat or open your wallet. *Give up catalog shopping for a while, and see how much money you don't spend.* How does it feel to give up that easy fix?

How about those expensive meals that didn't taste that great? And even if they did, what about cutting back for now? What if you and a couple of friends started cooking from time to time? Sure, you deserve to eat out and enjoy a meal, but you also deserve a future that offers you lots of the things that you truly want.

Make a list of the small things that bring you pleasure and joy. When you feel you need to go out and spend, get something from your list. Focus your attention on what really satisfies your need for immediate gratification and get one of those things. Make the purchase meaningful.

Tell other people about your new game plan. Other people get excited for you and their energy will help support you. *Focus on a plan.* Planning works. One day at a time, one decision at a time, and you're on your way out of the ghetto. Keep score; watch yourself winning.

Forget the credit cards but remember the credit—to yourself, for being willing to face the future.

Diets Don't Work

Diets don't work. They never have and never will!

Ever been on a diet, or know someone else who has? We start out all excited and enthusiastic. Even if we're not thrilled about the concept of giving things up, we're thrilled about looking different, about looking like that person we always knew we could be. Often the diet is triggered by an event or the upcoming season. Weddings do it for some, vacations or family reunions for others. Better yet, how about a school reunion with people you haven't seen in ten or even twenty-five years? Diet rules are tricky . . . something like underwear rules.

Spring and summer seasons act as strong catalysts for lots of people. The thought of putting on a pair of shorts or a bathing suit is enough to plunge them into the aisles of the local pharmacy, stocking up on liquid diet and high-fiber snack bars. Maybe that's why people in southern California stay slim. They always have nice weather and can be seen at the beach twelve months a year! But they are rarely satisfied with their size either, always longing to be just a little smaller in the waist and hips. They live the diet cycle too. It's hard to keep that nice steady weight; the yo-yo trap keeps snaring us. Sometimes we just can't fit into our old clothes or can't stand the thought of buying that next size up. Who likes doing that? But how long can you tell yourself that the store should carry higher-quality items and that Seventh Avenue is cutting things very skimpy this year?

If the diet is especially strict or very different from our usual diet, we are extra enthusiastic to start. You know the saying, "No pain, no gain." We get the new special foods from the store, read all about the preparation. We tell our friends, we declare our goals, we drink plenty of water, remember our vitamins and chew thirty times with each bite. We work the diet with our heart and soul. We have iced tea or bottled water while our friends drink that beer or Bloody Mary; we ask for our salad dressing on the side. We know all about carbohydrates and fat content and can quote to all interested, and uninterested, parties what they should know about their diets.

Some of us stop in the very first days. Some of us succeed at achieving our proclaimed goal, but after a long succession of "God, you look wonderful!" "How much weight have you lost?" "You look years younger," we notice that we are beginning to cheat. You know, just that half a piece of delicious chocolate, one glass of wine, or dinner at your mother's house.

Studies done over and over again by different groups report that the average American regains lost weight in the twelve months after the diet is complete. Not only do we gain back what we lose, but because our metabolic rates change with dieting, we often end up with more poundage than we started with. Then next season we are on to a new diet plan. This is known as the famous yo-yo dieting plan! So what's the deal?

The deal is that diets don't work. You have to work the diet! The programs directed at weight loss having the highest success ratios are those that support *rational behavior modification.* These programs can work. Of course, this assumes that the person on the plan can exhibit rational behavior. For purposes of this conversation we will go along with that theory. The plan is designed to allow you to live, breathe, be with other people while achieving your goals. You've seen what I'm talking about: If we use strict, intense, punishing diets, once most of us get to our initial goals—assuming we have hung in and fought the valiant fight—we stop. We get tired of doing without, of not having what we want on our tongues, of giving up the immediate gratification of that fattening but extraordinary cheesecake. We slide, we explain, we gain.

Money diets don't work either. Same theory. It's too hard for the most well-intentioned men or women to keep giving up what they love and adore. It's too hard to keep giving up things that feel important and needed. You can do it for a short time, but it's hard to feel hungry all the time for things that you have become accustomed to. It just can't be sustained.

Hey, everybody can bag lunch for a while. And most people go on money diets with the same vengeance they use for food diets. It starts like this: They have just read an article, visited their accountant or financial adviser, spoken to a friend, or looked at their bank and credit card statements, and decided that enough is enough. Perhaps they are getting ready for an event like buying a house, or expecting the birth of a child, or planning to start a business or retire from one. So they intend to take things in hand. New beginnings and all that. Then it happens. The diet, their resolution, piece by piece starts to unwind. It's too hard not to buy just that one great piece of electronic or sports equipment, too hard not to buy that special dress or take a taxi when it's late or raining. How can you go without a vacation after you've worked so hard all year? You're burned out and need to get away. Is that too much to give yourself? It's too painful to tell everyone at Christmas that you don't plan on exchanging expensive gifts, that you would like just to share the holidays. Are you willing to have them think that you don't care, or worse, that you have financial pressure? No way! And so the money diet goes to hell.

Not only do you notice that you swing right back to your old money habits, you often swing back twice as hard! Not a pretty picture. Before you started all this, you weren't doing half the damage you are now. Just like that old food diet. You just can't find a balance. Your very metabolism is off-kilter and it's playing havoc with your nervous system.

So then what? Please: DON'T DIET. *Don't suffer. Don't walk away in despair. There really is hope. You can win at this game, but only if you give up dieting.* No more starving, then binging. For some of you this may not seem interesting enough. I know, No pain, no gain. Well, I think that it ain't necessarily so.

Put together a list of all the money you spend and what you spend it on. Be specific.

Don't just note that you spent money for a night of entertainment; but break it down so you have a list that looks like this:

Movies $6
Candy $2
Restaurant $8
Gasoline $10

Here's some good news: Just by using lists as a way of following what you eat or spend, you will cut down consumption. Guaranteed.

When I first started working with clients, creating lists, I noticed that it was difficult to get people to be specific. "Where do you spend your money?" I would ask. "On Visa or MasterCard and American Express," they would often answer. As if these were consumer items! They meant it. Because they charged everything, the places they had bought from had become a blur. They started thinking of the vehicle that they used to purchase goods and services as the goods and services themselves.

Jot down the amount and place you have spent money in a daily planner.

Hold on to all your receipts.

Transfer all important information to a safe and permanent place.

Put all this information into categories.

A Category List looks like this:

HOUSEHOLD
rent/mortgage/maintenance
utilities: telephone, gas, electric,
heat
gardening
repairs
appliances
furniture

AUTOMOBILE/TRANSPORTATION
payments (purchase or lease)
gasoline
garage
repair
taxis
public transportation/rentals

ENTERTAINMENT
movies/theater
restaurants
cable/movie rental
purchase of TV, stereo, or any other appliance of this nature
entertainment at home (parties)
books/subscriptions

GIFTS
birthday
anniversary
special occasion
holiday

MEDICAL CARE
doctors
dentist
eyeglasses
prescriptions/nonprescription medication

CHILD CARE
school
baby-sitter
day care

CLOTHING
(for all family members)

TOILETRIES

PERSONAL CARE
haircuts, manicures, etc.

LAUNDRY/DRY CLEANERS

TAXES
income tax
real estate

FOOD

INSURANCE
life
health
disability
long-term care
homeowner's
automobile

PROFESSIONAL DUES

EDUCATION

PETS

VACATIONS

MISCELLANEOUS
(If you don't know where it goes, put it here.)

INVESTMENTS/SAVING

Keep updating your information, if you intend to be accurate. Don't wait to play catch-up and think that you're going to remember—your mind won't want you to know what you are doing with your money! After all, if you figure out what you have been doing, you just might start making changes.

This list should be a fair representation of one year of spending. If you have last year's canceled checks and consolidated year-end bills from credit card companies, use them to help jog your memory.

Carol was shocked to find out that last year she and her husband had spent over $20,000 on catalog purchases. A busy doctor with a full-time practice and two small children, she does shopping at night on the phone from catalogs.

If you like using your computer, you can buy programs at your local computer software store that can help you create these lists. There are books that can give you formats to follow if you prefer something different from the one in this chapter. It doesn't matter how you get this assignment done, so long as you get it done. If you find your-self spending a long time on figuring out how to do this, you are prob-ably just wasting time so that you can avoid getting to the matter at hand. This whole project is really not complicated. All you need is a pen and a paper; everything else is extra. As I said, the same process is used in dieting programs, where you keep lists to write down every-thing that you eat. This has two purposes. One is to raise your con-sciousness about what you are doing, the other is to give you a starting point. Foodwise, moneywise, it makes no difference, the principle is the same. The purpose of this exercise is to have a legible, correct list of your spending habits.

Calculate the percentages of each category you spend versus your income.

Easy, simple adding and dividing! Get your calculator. Nothing com-plicated here, so hang in there with me.

If you take home $36,000 a year after taxes are withheld from your paycheck and you spend $5,000 on one vacation and $1,000 on another, the math will look like this:

$$\$5,000 + \$1,000 = \$6,000 \text{ total spent}$$
$$\$36,000 \text{ (earned)} \div \$6,000 \text{ (spent)} = 6$$
$$1/6 = 16.5\%$$

Interpretation: you spend one-sixth, or 16.5 percent, of your available funds on vacations. *Did you realize this?*

Let's try another:

You have added all your receipts together and determined that you spend $12,000 on rent and household costs.

$$\$36,000 \text{ (earned)} \div \$12,000 \text{ (spent)} = 3$$
$$1/3 = 33.3\%$$

If you continue this process, at the end you will have determined not only the total dollars you have spent but also the percentage of the total each cost represents. Some of you may find the answer to how the bulging credit card balance keeps getting fatter and fatter.

You may notice that you are consuming more money than you are making. Ah, the magic of credit cards!

Now, you may ask, how do I calculate the gifts given to me by Aunt Ida or my lover? If I spend the money that I'm given from another source, where does all that figure in? Well, just remember to add in the gifts to your total income so that you will have a real picture of *all* the money that you have available. Income means *all* income, not just earned income. If you receive any dividends, interest, or gifts, they need to be counted. If you have rental income from property, it counts too. *Income is income.* Then just list the amount of money you spent on the trip, dress, or whatever in the same way with your other expenditures. Put it in the correct category that we've identified before. That way you won't mess up the calculations.

Example: You are lucky enough to inherit $5,000. You add it to your income of $45,000. You spend it on furnishings for your house.

$45,000 (earned) + $5,000 (gift) = $50,000
$50,000 ÷ $5,000 – 10
1/10 = 10% of total monies spent on home

What is a must and what is negotiable?

Taxes, I'm afraid, are a must. So is rent or maintenance. But where you live and how much you pay may or may not be negotiable. Eating is not negotiable; what you eat and where you eat may be. Got the picture?

Rational Behavior Modification 101: What are you willing to change in your spending habits?

Here's where honesty and reality come into play. What is possible and what is fantasy? Pick items that you will really be able to do something about. Do not make a huge, unattainable commitment and set yourself up to fail. This is just like the food diet, remember? If you deny yourself too much, you may feel deprived and rebel, reverting to the same money habits as before, or worse ones. Be honest about what you are really willing to do.

Fanny noticed that she and her boyfriend were spending a large percentage of their money on eating out. They decided this would be an easy place to cut back. Because they both have very late work schedules, they agreed that while they wouldn't stop eating out, they would be willing to give up the expensive bottle of wine with each meal! Dessert they would eat at home. No starvation diet for them.

Set short- and long-term goals . . . stay with the program.
Setting goals for yourself gives you a way to check how you are doing. Where would you like to be one year from now? Six months? One month? How are you going to get there?

David and Jennifer have two children and want to plan for their college educations. The boys are 3 and 4 years old. Their college is a *long*-term goal because it's fourteen years in the future.

When they calculated their spending habits they were surprised to see how much money was being spent on toys. They've decided to spend less money on toys and games, videos, and junk and instead put away $150 a month toward education planning. At the end of each year they will have saved $1,800 *(short-*term goal*)*. Sometimes the boys get money as gifts. David and Jennifer will take the cash and checks that they get on birthdays and holidays and put that money in the fund. When they shared this idea with the rest of their family, everyone was delighted. All the grandparents were happy to help them get ready for their kids' college. They realize the costs are high and they can make a difference. They still plan on having the pleasure of buying fun things for the grandchildren; but when they get the desire to splurge on toys, they'll *buy* a little and *save* a little.

By changing their ways of spending, David and Jennifer affected how their extended family members spent too. They also set their boys an eventual example of creating a game plan to accomplish long-term goals. The boys were given coin banks with a clear plastic front panel so as their coins were deposited they could see their money grow. They also got to determine what that money would be spent on in the future when the bank was full. Instead of buying candy, stickers, or small toys each time they were given money, they saved for something important. The whole family started enjoying doing this!

Work with a coach. If you have an accountant or financial adviser already, ask her if she would be willing to work with you to set your spending program in motion. If not, find out the names of advisers that friends or family work with. This is a great way to do business. Working with somebody else adds another dynamic to this game: *partnership. Teamwork is powerful.* Sometimes it's harder to keep a promise to yourself than to someone else. Sometimes it's hard to figure out what action needs to be taken first. Sometimes it's just hard to do all this alone. If this is the goal, if it's important to you, then set yourself up to win. GET HELP if that's what it will take to help you win.

Don't misunderstand when I say you may need help. I don't doubt you are capable and trustworthy. But everybody can use help in doing things they may never have done before. If you don't want to hire someone, then get somebody you know, somebody who will understand you and work in partnership to get you in shape financially. Someone who has, shall we say, his or her own financial house in order already.

Not too long ago I began to work out at the gym again. When I noticed that I wasn't keeping my promise to myself to go three times a week, I started to work with a trainer. You bet I show up for that.

Being an overspender, just like being an overeater, has nothing to do with how smart you are or even how capable you are. It has nothing to do with how well you understand the problem itself. You may be very smart and understand the problem all too well, and this has nothing to do with being a good person.

Set deadlines.

Set reasonable but realistic deadlines. Don't forget, you want to *win* at this. Setting deadlines to have information gathered and compiled works even better when you set the schedule with someone else. If they really are playing on your team, they'll hold you to your word. And we're less apt to break our word to others!

- Having someone else to ask for clarification when you don't understand what you are reading keeps you from getting bogged down.
- Having someone else look at the information makes it really real. It's hard to get vague when there's a witness.

Recently I met a young woman whom the world thinks of as very successful. She's 28 years old and by all standards she has it all. She and her lover live in an apartment where they both operate their own businesses. Susan is a photographer, Lisa an architect. They've been together since they met in college. Susan earns what they had thought was more than enough to do the things they like to do and go to the places they like to go. They have separate checking and savings accounts and credit cards in each name.

Every year Susan runs up extraordinary credit card bills around the Christmas holidays and takes three months to pay them off. Every year the credit card company increases her credit line because she's been such a good customer. Isn't life grand? Every year she vows not to spend so much this time. Every April she is shocked at how much she has to pay in taxes. She files quarterly because she's self-employed, but somehow every April she still owes more. Every year she and her accountant talk about the benefits of opening up a retirement account, and every year for the past six years she has opted not to do it yet because she just doesn't have the money. Every year she says that she needs to get lean and mean and start saving. Sort of like those of us who keep buying those elastic-waist pants and talk of hope for next spring's new wardrobe.

She and Lisa alternate paying for the restaurant bills or the food delivery every night. They share apartment costs and vacation costs. They never, ever have any extra money.

They have had discussions with each other ad nauseam about what terrible people they are! Nothing much has changed as a result of all that breast-beating. They have given up going out to eat for weeks on end. Then they swing back, and when they do the bills mount faster than before. What's a girl to do?

Remember, the first step is to sit down and figure out where you are spending your money. Lisa and Susan were getting very anxious. "You mean everything? That's going to make me very nervous," said Lisa. "Me too," said Susan.

If you start to become anxious while filling out the lists that identify where you spend your money, stop and take a deep breath. Now really look at the paper. If you cannot look at the paper, wait until you can. You waited this long; you'll wait a little longer. All we're doing is tracking how you consume your money instead of how you consume your food. Recall again that just keeping a list of what you eat helps you lose weight. This paper process with money works the same way. So, if you have so much anxiety related to this issue that breathing becomes a problem, stop what you are doing immediately and begin to take slow, even breaths. It is difficult to move on in this process if you are not breathing. *So breathe . . . and relax!*

Months later, after working on the lists that we had created, Susan and Lisa came back for another visit with me. Once they had calmed down and taken a few deep breaths, we were able to start talking.

"Now look at the papers in front of you," I said to them. "Where do you spend your single most concentrated amount of money, besides taxes? Is it for clothing, dining out, gifts, travel? What in this package would be the easiest for you to modify? Remember, don't throw away what you really cannot stand to give up. *Give up or modify what's easiest.* If taking a car service is important to you because of safety or convenience, don't give that up. Otherwise, you'll go for a week or two with public transportation, then rebel, probably blowing the entire plan."

Susan lives far from public transportation and when she needs to go see a client, she has to take all her equipment and her books. In a big city, that is a true pain in the neck. It would be not only cumbersome but unsafe for her to travel on subways and buses with lots of expensive equipment. Cutting back on car service would not be sensible for her. But she could make lunch every day in the office. Originally, she and Lisa had thought it would be great to keep their businesses completely separate from their home. They never walked into the kitchen during the day. They ordered lunch in. By looking at this situation more creatively Susan decided that she could make her lunch in the morning, leave it on the counter, and pick it up at lunchtime. That would save between $6 and $10 a day—that's $30 a week at a minimum, $1,500 a year if you figure on fifty weeks (the other two weeks they're on vacation). That could certainly go toward a retirement plan contribution. By sending a check once a month to her broker to invest, Susan could redirect the money before it disappeared as it had always done in the past.

She and Lisa could also probably eat in a couple of nights a week. They had gotten into the habit of eating out every night, mostly because they worked out of their house, but in truth both liked cooking. Just the bottle of wine at dinner was a big savings when they drank it at home instead of in a restaurant. They each could cook one night. They might even get to like just hanging out, the way they used to. This solution wasn't too different from what Fanny and her boyfriend had chosen to do. Spending a high percentage of money on eating out seems to be a theme that shows up for busy people. With some modification, costs can be reduced without the experience of being punished or starved to death. *What a concept: no punishment!*

There was no point at looking at the money spent on Christmas gifts for family. Neither Lisa nor Susan was open to making any concession about holiday time. But the women decided that they could adjust the gifts they bought each other. By cutting the amount they spent on each other in half, they would be ahead and still have the pleasure of exchanging gifts—although Susan says that it is really hard for her not to splurge. She and Lisa have made a pact to cut gift costs at least 20 percent this year and increase the amount saved every year in the future. What a deal! We'll see.

Walk a Dog, Get a Wife

My Aunt Frances always had strong feelings on the subject of money. You may recall that she and my Uncle Mac lived in the projects on Avenue X. They were the ones with plenty of sour pickles on the plate and Ebinger's cakes in their kitchen.

My Aunt Fran is my mother's sister and I adore her. She always worried that she'd outlive her money, chafed when my uncle was what she considered overly generous, and fretted over what others might not even notice. Of course, she thought she was just being responsible. She was monetarily responsible all the time, as far back as I can remember. She paid her bills on time, never overspent, and worried, worried, worried. Reaching her sixties, she noticed that her memory was going. She and Uncle Mac were living in Florida at the time. She asked me if she could visit me in New York and if I would take her to a doctor to see what was wrong. Aunt Fran was very frightened. She thought her children might be taking money from her and she wanted me to promise that I'd protect her. Money paranoia, as we now know, can be one of the symptoms of Alzheimer's disease. Of course, I agreed to the visit.

Anyway, when they came to New York, I made an appointment for her at Long Island College Hospital with a neurologist who had been referred to me. It's close to my home. Aunt Fran wanted me to take her there alone. She said that my Uncle Mac could drop us off but that he couldn't go into the doctor's office with us—in fact, she would rather he stayed home. In one of our quiet times alone together she told me she thought Uncle Mac wouldn't understand her fear about money. The irony is was that my aunt and uncle had joint accounts all their lives. They never had what would be considered very much, and they'd shared whatever they had. My uncle is an honest man and never made a financial decision without consulting Aunt Fran, and my cousins Steve and Alan never asked one question about their parents' financial affairs. These facts, however, meant very little to my aunt, who was feeling very agitated. Uncle Mac did drive us to the hospital and although he wanted to speak with the doctor, he honored my aunt's wishes, waiting for us in the car right outside.

The doctor was very gracious and listened to everything my aunt told him. He asked lots of questions, poked and prodded her, had her touch her toes and her nose, and when it was all over he said, "I'm not sure. I don't know if in fact this is Alzheimer's; I don't want to label anything too early, and there is nothing definitive here. She's depressed and worried—that's not unusual for her age and her generation." He said that I should tell Uncle Mac that he suggested couples counseling, although he added that he really didn't see most couples taking that path at this stage in life. There was no way I could picture Aunt Fran and Uncle Mac in counseling either. What she really needed was TLC, gentleness, understanding, conversation, and partnership. The doctor gave her some medication for her restlessness and agitation, wished us luck, and waved us good-bye.

When we got home my poor uncle was nervous. "What did the doctor say?" I told him, while my aunt listened too, very concerned about my response. "He said her financial fears were not unusual for your generation, having been brought up during the Depression and all; she appears to be depressed too. He gave us a prescription to fill that should help her anxiety at night so the two of you can get some rest." I continued. "He recommends tenderness and special care. The doctor said that she needs warmth and love to survive this." My aunt stood on the sidelines smiling. This was the first time that we all openly acknowledged that there was a problem, that she had an illness.

It took three more years until there was a definitive diagnosis of Alzheimer's. My Uncle Mac has been very devoted to my aunt since the onset of her illness, never wavering in his commitment to make her life as good as possible. Days have been hard, but he never fails to get a big smile on his face when he talks about the prescription I said that the doctor had given us that day.

Aunt Fran and Uncle Mac have two sons, Steve and Alan. Steve is the older and as a kid he was always pampered. He was my aunt's eighth pregnancy, and the first one to survive, so needless to say, in our family it was like the birth of Christ. He got into trouble as a kid, and later on in his early adult life too.

I really love Steve. He was my favorite playmate when we were small. He's got a heart of gold, but in his early days he was very irresponsible. I won't go into the "why" of things or the "what could have been done." Let's just say he never appeared to have learned about responsibility. At least, financial responsibility was not a topic of conversation with him. By the time Aunt Fran got sick, she and Uncle Mac had already moved to Miami. Steve was on his own. He had been living in his own place for years, but hardly, as they say, made a living. He always kept a job, but having a career was not his focus back then. My aunt and uncle were always bailing him out, hoping that someday he would grow up.

Sometime in his late thirties my cousin's financial umbilical cord was really stretched. My aunt was ill, my uncle preoccupied, and my cousin reached a turning point. Steve decided to become a responsible person at last. He told me that he had just decided it was time. Who knows, perhaps it was the realization that his parents could no longer care for him, or perhaps it was plain old maturity. In any case, he and a friend took an apartment to share in Forest Hills. He had been living in a converted basement apartment in a neighborhood that was not really conducive to any kind of social life. Things were changing. He was happy and excited about the new move. He went to a pound and picked out a dog to take home and care for. Steve told me he thought this was a good way to start proving to himself that he could be a responsible person. He began to save money. When Alan's wife gave birth, Steve thought seriously enough to buy the baby some shares of stock, an idea he would never have thought of before. Things were looking up. We said he was becoming a mensch.

The best part of this story is yet to come. Steve loved his dog, and she loved him. He walked her every day on time, and when he was home from work they took extra special trips to the park. One day while he was walking her he met a very nice woman named Linda, who was also walking her dog. They became friends. She has an adorable daughter named Sara who often walked their dog too. Soon Steve, Linda, Sara, and the two dogs all fell in love.

Steve made a nice proposal, and he, Linda, Sara, and the two dogs got married. They had a wedding and all moved into a big apartment.

My Uncle Mac was overwhelmed with joy. My Aunt Fran was in a nursing home by now, but she was still capable of understanding that things were changing for her son. No one had thought that walking a dog would have such extraordinary results.

Uncle Mac decided that it would bring him a lot of pleasure to give some of his money to his children so that they could buy a home. He didn't want them to have to wait for something to happen to him and Aunt Fran. He felt that she would approve. So Uncle Mac made arrangements to give Steve and Linda a wedding gift. It made everyone happy. All Uncle Mac had to do was ask the accountant to file papers on his behalf letting the government know that he and Aunt Fran had given away more than $10,000 each to Linda and Steve. It would be counted toward their estate later.

Steve now has what he never even thought possible in those days long ago. He pays taxes and trims a lawn. He visits the accountants, has learned about paying points on a mortgage, and has even bought homeowner's insurance. He says that someday he may even vote Republican.

Somehow Steve didn't think he needed to be responsible while his mom and dad were close or capable of taking care of him. He'd never thought of living life any other way. When he was nearing that magical, mysterious 40, maybe his age kicked in. Whatever the motivation, *RESPONSIBILITY* became his watchword for the nineties.

Money has the power to confer self-esteem. It is a way of showing ability, adjustment, responsibility, and maturity. It weaves in and out of every family web. Who would deny its strength?

Moving On

Did you ever hear someone say, "I need my space"? Have you ever thought it yourself? Though it's an expression most frequently associated with intimate relationships, today as more parents and their adult children are living together, these words take on special meaning.

You know I have two sons. Andrew, the younger one, is almost 25 years old now. He lived in Portugal on and off for two years. He had gone there to paint, learn the language, experience life. He had moved on. Then he decided to come home again for a while.

When he left to live abroad he told me that he was really moving out this time. I'll bet you have said things like that yourself, or known someone who has. The twenties are a very exciting time of life, full of new beginnings, a time when anything seems possible. My son had moved out to live away at college, but this was different. He was changing his life as well as his zip code. He was back but moving on. Of course, this will always be his home and regardless of where I live there will always be a place for him. But I knew what he meant. It was his time to be independent, to go it alone. We were both really going it alone. He hadn't been living home much, but it had been his base. Now, he was planning on getting a different mailing address.

The memory of moving out of my parents' home is still vivid. It feels like I left home yesterday . . . and a million years ago. When I moved to Philadelphia after graduating from nursing school, I thought I was moving out of my parents' home for good. When I decided to return to New York, I came back to my parents, but now it was very different for me. I had experienced being an adult, taking on responsibility for myself. While I was out on my own, there had been no rules to follow except the ones that I made. Nobody told me when to do the laundry, or where to shop, or how to spend my money. But when I came home I knew that no matter how grown up I felt now, regardless of my life experience, I was once again a child in my folks' home. That's the way it is. When parents and kids are living together the parents can't help but feel that they are in charge. No matter how old the child is (my parents still treat me this way from time to time), the child is a child to the parent. And no matter how emotionally emancipated I like to think I am, I operate the same way.

So when Andrew called to tell me that he was coming home again, I could imagine his feelings about moving back in. This was definitely not his first choice; it was the most reasonable choice, it was the most economical one, but psychologically it was not the best choice—not for either of us. And we both knew it.

Sometimes something as insignificant as having a house painted can be symbolic. You know how you plan certain things based on what's happening with the kids? Well, it so happens that I had postponed having my apartment painted until Andrew moved out. It's not that I had thought he would upset my plan; it was just a "new beginning" that felt right to me. The rooms would be changed. The painter had been hired, the colors were selected, and I was about to have the work done when Andrew called to say that he was coming back to New York. He was coming home. He had visited once before while he was away, but now he was moving back in to live with me again for a while. He had been gone only six months this time and he was coming back home.

I am a good mother. I love my son. I would kill for him. But just weeks earlier I had made a decision to turn Andrew's room into a study for myself. It was part of the "new beginning" program that I had undertaken. I had thought about it for a while; it was a tough decision. After all, his room was his room and I didn't want my son to think he wasn't welcome. On the other hand, he had moved out and said he was not coming home. I did want to take his feelings into consideration, so I discussed it with him on the phone during one of the weekly conversations that we had while he was away. He had no problem with it at all. He told me not to worry about his feelings. At that point he was out and planned to stay out. No need to keep his old room the way it had been. I felt a little guilty when I began to move his things into boxes, but I decided to go for it anyway. He had assured me that he was staying in Portugal and he had no plans to return to the States.

What delight I had felt in having so many closets to use, spreading all my clothing into the closet in Andrew's old room! That closet would be reserved for off-season clothing. My own closet would hold only what I was using now. So much space for just one person—it felt fabulous. I felt like a wealthy woman—well, not wealthy, but abundant, slightly spoiled.

That's when Andrew's call came: just as the painter was finished, the pictures were hung, the desk and furniture were in their new den. Can't you just picture my face? Should I move my things out of his closet? Should I put everything back into my old closet space? I decided to wait and see what his plans were when he got here. We hadn't discussed much about that on the phone. The day he arrived back in New York I felt bad about his not having his room, which I felt rightfully belonged to him. On the ride back from the airport I made a point of reminding him not to be shocked that his room did not exist anymore. Apparently he didn't care. Either that or he was very generous. "Mom," he said, "I'm not staying for long at your place. I'm just staying long enough to save money to get my own apartment."

He moved into the small bedroom, now designated for guests, and unpacked. The next day he started looking for a job. He was totally committed to earning money and moving out. One week later he started his new job. When he called to ask for advice on how many deductions to declare for withholding tax on his paycheck, I suggested he take one. That should cover his taxes without having too much withheld from his pay. He offered to call my accountant; actually, he preferred to. He was starting to handle things on his own. He asked for the telephone number. He wanted to be sure that he wouldn't have to pay money the next April. I gave him the telephone number. No problem. It turned out that what I had said was true, but he wanted to hear it from the man himself. It was his money and he was in charge.

Now I'd like to share a little secret with you about my son. I love him very much. He's a really great guy. I always thought he was smart, handsome, kind, and wonderful to be with. I didn't always think he was very responsible, and in fact that may have been true about the Andrew who moved away—but that was not the Andrew who came home. He was transforming before my very eyes.

We went out for dinner and he told me his game plan. He was moving out within the next ninety days. Hopefully sooner, but it would definitely be no longer than three months before he was out again. He and his friend James from college were going to share an apartment. They were contacting real estate brokers and looking at places that they could afford. Impressive!

I had been noticing other changes. Every morning at about seven-thirty I get ready for work. When Andrew told me that he would be leaving at seven-thirty I cringed inside. I remembered the days when I would have to wake him three times for school. But every day he got up, ironed his clothing if necessary, and left for work on time. I'm sure he did the same in Portugal. I just wasn't there, and because it didn't happen in front of me I continued to see him in the light of the past. People grow up. He's a grown-up.

One day he called my office to find out how **direct deposit** works. He had decided that it would be best if he made arrangements for his employer to deposit his paycheck electronically directly into his checking account. That way he wouldn't risk losing the check or not being able to get to the bank on time to cash it. What's more, he would get interest on his money right away and not have to wait until the check cleared. With direct deposit the money is deposited as cash so there is no waiting time for a check to clear; you can use the funds immediately. Actually, I do the same thing with my paycheck. It was interesting for me to see the transition that Andrew had made into the world of money. His money was now a serious matter. He was in charge.

At dinner the next night Andrew told me about where he and James were looking for apartments, how much money they had figured they could spend, and showed me his basic budget. Go Andrew! They knew that if they got an apartment through a real estate agent they would have to pay the agent, plus a month's rent and a month's security deposit. They had also figured in the cost of a telephone hookup and the probability of deposits to the phone and electric companies. It looked as if they were running things tight, but would be on schedule if they kept to their budget. I offered to lend them some money. Andrew accepted after discussing it with James, but only on the condition that I set up a repayment plan and consider it a short-term loan. I was impressed.

Within six months' time, Andrew ended up making the decision to move out of New York again. The cost of living was too high for him to find a place where he could live and paint. He has moved to Philadelphia, not far from New York, where he lives alone. He single-handedly found an apartment, dealt with the real estate agent, turned on his utilities, and found a new job. It allows him to paint, which is his main focus. He has created a space for himself.

What I find extraordinary is that he has taught himself about money management and has it down to a science. It's not that I don't think my son is capable; of course I know he is. But he's my son, who left here a boy and returned a man, and I'm being called upon to realize that he wants to handle his finances for himself. It gives him a sense of self-respect. He feels good about what he's accomplishing and I feel good for him.

I also feel good for me. I feel safer knowing that he's going to be okay. I just sat down with him and talked about giving him power of attorney for my own accounts that have cash or securities in them. That way I know that if anything happened and I couldn't write a check or pay bills, he could do it for me. Imagine: *my son could take care of me!*

I also showed him where my **living will** is located. A legal document that can be created by an attorney, a living will defines what you may or may not want done to sustain your life if you are in an irreversible, terminal condition. Finally, I've given him a list of the telephone numbers of my accountant, lawyer, and trustee for my will. I've done the same thing with Jonathan. *It's very important that somebody have this information,* especially when you are single. Andrew sees this as my vote of confidence in him. And that's what it is.

I've visited his new place in Philadelphia. He's still working on it. It's wonderful. He's carving out his space and his life. I'm happy that he sees he can be in charge of his life. I'm proud that I helped in the growth and maturity of this man.

I'm also happy that I don't have to give up my closet space.

Facts We Learned:

RESPONSIBILITY

Saving credit card receipts is critical in the event of a dispute.

Direct deposit saves time by having money deposited as cash directly into your account.

Savings bond interest is not tax free . . . it is tax deferred.

Student loan and consumer interest charges are not tax deductible.

Living wills are used to define your wishes about health and finance in the event you cannot speak on your own behalf.

Lessons We Learned:

RESPONSIBILITY

Partnership can be a valuable asset: you don't need to do things alone.

Diets don't work . . . don't punish yourself.

Do yourself a favor and give yourself credit.

You can't hold anyone else responsible for your life but YOU.

IV.

SECURITY

SECURITY

1. Being secure means _____.

2. The things that would make me financially secure are _____.

3. When I feel secure my life is _____.

4. When I feel insecure my life is _____.

5. When I need to review my finances I _____.

6. What people don't know about me and money is _____.

Security

Do you feel safe, protected
and fine?
or
*Do you worry 'bout money
and not enough time?*

What is it that helps you feel
secure?
What can you do to make you feel sure?

Do you have a plan, are you
in charge of the game?
*Or do the days and years pass and
are things still the same?*

Gender Bias

I remember well the year the first man walked on the moon. It was 1969, the year my son Jonathan was born. Seems just like yesterday. Jonathan is married now and lives in Saskatchewan, Canada with his wife, Inger, and their two kids. Tyler is 6, Tiana is 2 years old. My children have been my greatest teachers and my grandchildren continue the lessons.

When I was bringing up my sons I never realized that I, the emancipated and liberated mother, financial adviser, and women's advocate, was guilty of gender bias. I expected my boys to be sensitive, loving men. They weren't permitted to have toy guns or watch violent movies or TV shows. I taught them to cook and make their beds. Andrew, my younger son, took dance class, and they both knew how to sew. My boys would be well rounded, knowing life at its fullest.

Once I started working on Wall Street, every year at Hanukkah I bought each of them one or two shares in a stock that they could identify with, like Disney or the telephone company. When they got dividend checks quarterly, they could spend the money any way they liked. So they learned something about the stock market and managing money. I even ran classes in their school to explain what a stock was. These classes, composed of both boys and girls, were taught how to follow the prices of stocks in the newspapers—practicing fractions at the same time—as they observed the daily rises and falls by halves and quarters and eighths.

Over the years I was delighted to see that these young men, my sons, had learned to respect girls and treat them fairly. They had been taught, as well as experiencing firsthand by living with me, that men and women are equal.

When Tyler, my first grandchild, was born, I was determined to start putting away money for his college education from the very beginning. I hadn't had the opportunity to do this for my boys, and believe me, it wasn't easy coming up with their tuition in big chunks when the time came. So now, while I can help plan for the future by putting away some money for Tyler, I do. Jonathan and Inger work very hard. They are having to do some financial juggling to make a go of their life together. Inger is still in school earning her degree in psychology, and plans to continue through to her doctorate. She makes the honors list every year. Jonathan has just started a business, which is doing well, but new businesses eat money. The business is run from their home and that makes it nice for all of them.

There's never extra money. Recently there was a dental emergency for Tyler that cost $300. Who would ever imagine one little 6-year-old visiting Doctor Dan could run up a bill like that? Good thing he put the tooth under the pillow and got a dollar back from the tooth fairy. Most people are shocked at the costs of bringing up their children, even though they think they're prepared. Nothing ever prepares you for kid costs.

At the same time that you are paying for nursery, day care, baby-sitters, and Gymboree, it would be best to also start saving for college. Of course, the best time to start saving for a child's college fund is the day the child is born, because then the money has an opportunity to really grow. The problem is that with all the money it takes just to nurture and care for a baby from day one, it can be downright difficult to include college planning too.

I decided this was something I could do almost painlessly for Tyler. I wanted to help start putting away college money for him now. I figured it out: I would put away $100 a month—which averages out to a little more than $3 a day—with no problem at all. Even if money grows at just 7 percent, it will double in ten years. The joy of compounding! It's a lot easier to put away money monthly than to come up with the big sums later. This kind of planning also yields a sense of security. It enables us to see the money growing and realize that committed, continual participation works. It just keeps adding up. This advice pertains to everybody, no matter how comfortable they are financially. Planning makes things work out better. It also helps us feel that we've done something about the future in case all our other best-laid plans don't take shape. People do lose their health, their wealth, their partners, and everything they were planning on doing or having may need to be rearranged. Of course, we don't expect these things to happen to us; we just know in the back of our minds that it's possible, and we protect ourselves the best ways that we can.

I made the decision to invest Tyler's money in mutual funds. I started by picking an aggressive growth fund. **Aggressive stock funds** invest in smaller companies that have a high growth potential over the years. However, they can be volatile and are best used when there is substantial time available for investing. Good for someone like Tyler who will need the money for college. These funds are professionally managed and allow an investor like me to participate in a diversified portfolio with small amounts of money. As Tyler gets older, I may switch some of this money into something less risky, but at his young age, with time on our side, I started with an aggressive stock fund. And by putting money into the account on the fifteenth of every month, I took the emotion out of making my decision. The mutual fund company was instructed to invest the money whether the stock market was up, down, or sideways. People use this same arrangement to have money taken from their paychecks to invest in their retirement accounts. This style of investing is also called **dollar cost averaging.** Because you make investments on many different days (let's say each month on the fifteenth) twelve times a year, the price of your purchase evens out over the long run, with your cost being neither the highest nor the lowest. I love this concept. I started by putting in $100 a month for Tyler and now he has over $7,000. I have also diversified some of his money by buying three other funds. One is a blue chip stock fund, one is a moderate growth stock fund, and the other is an international fund. Not only does he get diversification by owning a professionally selected and managed mutual fund portfolio, but he has four of them, so the money is allocated to different degrees of risk too. Way to go, Grandma York! (He calls me Grandma York. That's because I'm from New York. This is a very bright child!)

When Tiana was born I had never thought about whether I

wanted them to have a girl or a boy. I just wanted to have another healthy baby. My family has lots of boys—my brother Steve has three sons, I have two sons, and my son had a son. Pink is cute, but they make lots of great clothes for boys too. But this time we would have a little girl in our family.

I went to the store and bought lots of pink. It was a novelty. They make those crazy headbands for bald babies, and I bought some. She was a preemie, born seven weeks early, so we needed really tiny clothes. No problem; I found them too. You just have to know where to shop. I don't particularly like to shop, but I found I do love to shop for tiny pink garments. I ordered a silver spoon for Tiana just like the one I had gotten Tyler, and then I went to the jeweler's to order a small ring with the initial *T* engraved on it. I made sure that it had a small diamond chip too. It thrilled me to know that I had bought her first jewelry.

Not until weeks later did I realize that I had not given one thought to Tiana's investment account! I had not even considered a mutual fund or a savings bond. It wasn't the worst crime in the world, but it brought my consciousness to a screeching halt. With all of my advocacy for women, I too had placed my sweet granddaughter in a jewelry first, finances second mode.

I am happy to report that my momentary mental lapse in priorities has been repaired and Tiana now has her own mutual fund account just like her older brother Tyler. She also has a ring with a diamond and some very fine and gauzy pink-and-white clothing. One thing has nothing to do with the other.

My projections suggest that by the time Tiana and Tyler go to Harvard or Yale or study in Europe, the cost for four years of education will be around $50,000 a year. The cost of tuition at private colleges has gone up more than 150 percent since 1980—from $8,000 then to $20,000 in 1995. If you don't believe me, call Harvard and ask them what they project the future tuition to be in the year 2010 or so. When I went to Brooklyn College in 1964, my parents paid $12 a term, $24 a year. And I lived at home—there was no living on campus. My brother Steve, who is four years younger, paid about $12 a credit. We took an average of sixteen credits a term, so that meant $416 a year. Books and other lab supplies were not included. My son Andrew went to the state university. His basic cost of tuition plus room and board was about $7,000 a year. No books, no lab or other supplies here either; those were extra. He did get to live in a dorm with a zillion other kids. All told, college at the state university averaged about $12,000 a year—about 1,000 times what my parents paid for me at a comparable campus. Even if you exclude room and board, the costs of education have skyrocketed and will continue to outpace inflation. It's really valuable to take all this information seriously if you have planning to do for one or more children. At least I do!

Tyler and Tiana raise my level of consciousness. Even at these tender ages they remind me that men and women are both different and the same. They make me acutely aware of what I already knew: that planning for the future starts today and children deserve planning too—girls as well as boys!

Security Blanket

Close your eyes. Now picture yourself feeling completely safe and taken care of. You have everything you will ever need financially. All the money you've always wanted to have is yours. You can do and be anything you want. So what's the result? What would you be doing? What does your life look like in this world where you are everything and have everything that you want? How do you feel?

Do you often dream about what life would be like if you had more money? Wouldn't it be wonderful to win the lottery or have the people from Publishers Clearing House knock at your door? Wouldn't it be nice to get a call from a lawyer telling you that some rich old aunt or cousin you never met had left you loads of money?

What would life be like then? Would you quit your job, go back to school, donate money to charity, travel, buy a new home? Would you shop till you dropped? Then what would you do? Would you be happy?

Here is some sad news. Statistics tell us that most people who come into large sums of money often spend, lose, or give away one-third of it in the first year. Sometimes that's a very substantial amount. They just seem to have the money, and then . . . they don't. What happens?

What happens is that somehow they don't feel that the money is really theirs. *They don't take ownership of the money.* Sometimes they feel guilty about having so much while others around them have less. They feel that they have to say yes to every family member and friend who reaches out to them. Sometimes they just plain don't know just what to do.

If money is a metaphor in our lives, it is also an opportunity. We can use it as a teacher to help us understand who we are and how we operate. And what a teacher it can be!

Don't you know people who have money and yet are unfulfilled and dissatisfied? This couldn't be, if money were all it took to make people happy. Some lottery winners interviewed long after they've won have even expressed the wish that their apparent good fortune had never struck. In fact, strangely, there is a rather high suicide rate among lottery winners. Sociologists guess that these winners had thought money would change their lives, so much so that all the things that had made them unhappy would just disappear. Perhaps the disappointment of reality proved to be more than they could bear. Having money does not make life perfect. Ironically, what it can do is take the burden and pressure off us sufficiently to realize this truth.

One thing I notice when I talk to people who've inherited, won, or even begun to earn much more money than they had in the past is that their perception of money changes. What once was a dream now becomes part of day-to-day existence. Life itself becomes routine once again.

Lynne started singing in her church choir when she was 7 years old. By the time she was 16 she was sure that she wanted to be a professional singer more than anything in the world. She came from a poor family in Alabama, with no money for anything but the most basic necessities. Her brothers and sisters laughed at her when she told them that one day she would pack up and go to New York to make records. They knew the truth, and the truth was that nobody from their family was going anyplace. But Lynne's mother told her daughter to go after her dreams. When she combed her daughter's hair to get her ready for church choir she would whisper to her, "You hold on to your dreams now, honey, you hold on." And she did.

At 18, right after graduating from the local high school, Lynne packed her bags and came to New York City. That was ten years ago. When I met her she was singing and in fact had made a name for herself in the music business. Over the years she had hired a manager and an accountant. Two of her sisters were working for her. She had bought and sold two homes, unable to pay the large mortgages that she had taken on, and was living in a rented apartment. She had owned five cars—one for herself, the others for her family. She had gold and platinum credit cards from every major credit card company, and owed all of them money. She had paid off her parents' mortgage and sent her younger sisters to college. She now owed the IRS thousands of dollars in back taxes. She had made special arrangements with them to make monthly payments. In the meantime, the interest on all of her bills was mounting. Her accountant had tried to advise her and so had her manager. In fact, so had the manager and accountant she had before them. She was starting to get scared. No matter what she earned there was never enough, and the cycle was getting worse.

When Lynne came to see me, the first thing we did was talk for over an hour, trying to clarify what was going on. Did she in fact want things to change permanently, or was she looking for a Band-Aid? How much was she willing to do to have things be different? Sometimes we feel more secure being where we are than where we think we want to be. Lynne was going to have to take a hard look at what had made her choose her behavior.

Sometimes we do want to be elsewhere but we don't want to do the work it would take to get us there. We willingly give up the big win for temporary good feelings along the way. You know what I mean: I'd like to be a size 5 again but I'm not willing to give up eating any sweet food, so my chances of actually being size 5 don't look too promising. The same thing happens with money. If you want things to be different, then you have to be willing to behave differently; otherwise there is no way out—no matter how many advisers, coaches, and managers you get, you'll find a way to sabotage your success.

I want you to know that Lynne is a very smart woman. This has nothing to do with being smart. As a matter of fact being smart can even be a problem! The smarter we are, the more easily we can figure out ways to get into a mess, and some of us are truly creative. But it is also true that if your brains and creativity got you where you are, they can probably get you out. You just need to decide if you want out.

First: Remember all the other times you've handled things. This is just another one of those times.

Second: Look at the whole picture. What advice would you give a friend in the same situation?

Third: Begin at the beginning. Create a game plan.

Fourth: Start doing things. Some things can be done right away. You'll start to feel momentum building.

Fifth: Give yourself credit for everything you are doing to make things change. Give yourself lots of pats on your back, and it will fuel your energy to keep going!

That's just what Lynne did. Here's how.

She was very worried about her credit. She was sure she had messed things up so badly that she would never have any credit again. One of the first things she agreed to do was to get an outside credit-reporting company immediately to do a credit check on herself. For a fee, these companies will provide you with your own credit report. It took just a few minutes to start this process and was almost painless.

Getting the report in the mail a few weeks later made Lynne slightly woozy. Before she opened it, she was sure that she was blacklisted forever. It turned out that although she owed a lot money, she had never defaulted on her payments or even paid late. Somehow she had thought that because she had been paying only her minimum balances and still using her card, she would show as a bad credit risk. Not so: as long as she was making timely payments, that was good enough for the credit card companies. Her credit rating was just fine. She needed to work on paying off the cards, but that had nothing to do with her credit rating. If anything, it made her a good credit risk for the future, because it showed a long history of making her payments. She had been nervous about getting the report, but now she was glad she'd gotten it. Reading the report in black-and-white print made her feel safer and more hopeful about the future.

We talked about how she'd gotten into this state of financial distress and tried to identify the recurrent themes. Lo and behold, there they were:

"All my life my parents worked hard for me and my brothers and sisters and I wanted to pay them back. It seemed so easy for me and so hard for them all back there at home. I just wanted to help. Besides all of that, I guess I wanted to prove them wrong and show that, after all, I had made it in the music business. Part of it was plain old showing off. The other thing I realize is that I really never touched the money. Somebody paid my bills and handled my affairs. It never seemed very real. I'm the only one who's ever going to write the checks from here on in. That'll keep me closer to reality."

This was a good start. But only a start. In order for Lynne to change things, she needed more than this understanding of herself and how she had behaved in the past; she needed to do something about it. It's easier to take charge of your checkbook than to change a pattern of behaving toward family. That would be the real test. Would she be willing to give up the good feelings she got from being generous to all those people? That was a really tough one. What would they think of her now?

"I know that this is going to be very hard. I think my sisters and brothers are going to be angry with me. I'll bet my parents understand, but my siblings . . . that's another story. I'm just going to have to be brave. It makes me very nervous to think of having this talk with them, but I just know it's bad for all of us the way it is now. Besides, I can't go on this way."

Lynne's family had started to depend on her. They had even begun to take her for granted. It had become a given that Lynne would be the security blanket for them all. Withdrawing all the financial assistance was going to be no easy road. But it could be the beginning of a new way for all of them.

It took a couple of months. Lynne made a trip home to Alabama and spoke to everybody. She says that she was sick for days before the visit, feeling very selfish about having to stop giving as much as she had in the past. She was worried that her family wouldn't want to talk to her, that they'd be angry. I understand. Sometimes when I have to say no it makes me uncomfortable too—downright guilty at times. There is a well-known book called *When I Say No, I Feel Guilty*. This is not a new theme in human history.

It turned out that everybody was more understanding than she'd expected. Often things work out that way. Don't confuse that with being delighted! In no way were her siblings pleased. But they did understand. The cars had to be sold first; then they would talk about what other changes had to happen.

Since the cars had been fully paid for, Lynne could sell them and use the money to pay off her back taxes. That was a relief. Now that she was no longer hemorrhaging money, she could start to focus on the other things, like paying off her credit card debt, moving to a larger apartment so she could have the extra bedroom for a studio, and maybe even saving some money. Talk about feeling secure—she felt as if she could start breathing again.

The next time we met we focused on what would be important to Lynne in creating her new security blanket: a savings plan, hiring someone to take care of her office, retirement planning. It takes conscious effort not to backtrack. But things are beginning to work out for this talented singer, and the more they work out, the more reinforcement she feels, the better shot she has at staying with the new game.

It's funny how Lynne got a new sense of security in finding out that her family still cared about her, and that she could turn her life around. In the beginning she thought money was her security, but it's the sense that she can *handle* money that gives her real security now.

A Matter of Perception

Ever put a puzzle together? At first you can't figure out anything; the entire tabletop looks like a hodgepodge of junk. Then you step back and notice how the pieces should fit. Sometimes it's just a matter of moving them around. Sometimes you need to put down the piece you're holding and start with another one.

We laid out all the information on the desk. That way we both could look at everything and start to put together a list of all Caryn's assets and liabilities.

Caryn's been a schoolteacher at a New York City junior high school since she got out of college eighteen years ago. She's single. She works extra hours tutoring kids after school and loves her students. But she's getting stressed with her work. She feels trapped in a very plain, economically unfulfilling lifestyle. There's no question that being a teacher offers some nice benefits, like short days, long summer vacations, and holidays off. But it doesn't pay that well. So, if a person wants to have more, it takes more money. In order to get more money you have to work more at other things. That's why Caryn tutors three nights a week.

About three years ago Caryn bought a co-op, using all her savings as a down payment. Now she struggles to pay her mortgage, her maintenance, her car loan, her student loan, and her small but very annoying credit card bills and still have some money left over for socializing. Her sister just had twins and named Caryn as godmother: an honor, a privilege, and a very substantial additional cost!

I'm sure you can identify with those wonderful double-edged moments. The gift, the party, the restaurant bill—all for very good reasons, but painful nevertheless.

The way Caryn talked, her situation sounded pretty pitiful. The way she saw it, prosperity and abundance would never make it to her doorstep.

Honestly, when we started talking, Caryn looked like an old lady ready to pack it in. "There's no hope," she said, and she really meant it. You can tell when someone isn't joking. She wasn't joking. Life was looking bleak.

"Of course there's hope: you make $65,000 a year between your regular job and your tutoring. You are far from destitute." I smiled as we spoke. She didn't smile back. Did you ever have one of those moments when you try to be a cheerleader, someone's champion, and they just stare at you in disbelief that you could be right? This was one of those moments. I was feeling the heaviness in the air. This woman was not happy.

"I haven't gone clothes shopping in years," she told me. "I just lost some weight so I decided to go to Macy's and buy myself this new skirt—but other than that, nothing. I use my tutoring money to pay off my old bills. I don't want to create any new ones. My father and mother lived in debt all their lives. I don't want to repeat their mistakes."

"Why would you repeat their mistakes?" I asked her. "You are not your father and mother; you may have some traits like them, but you are not them. What did they do that got them into so much financial trouble?"

"My mother didn't work and my dad was a real easygoing guy. He never earned much—he was a bus driver. He got a good pension when he retired, but as far as earning a living went, he wasn't a big wage-earner. The thing is that they were always borrowing and owing everybody. We were four kids and they always wanted us to have the best. They couldn't afford the best, but they bought it anyway. It always made me nervous as a kid growing up, hearing them talk about how they would pay the bills, who they would and wouldn't pay. I feel very insecure about money all the time. No matter how much I talk to myself, I can't get rid of the feeling. I just want to know how bad things are, that's all."

So we began to look together. I'd mailed her a form but she hadn't completed it. It was as if everything was too much to handle. She did at least bring her bills and her papers, so we could go through them together. We listed all the bills, the totals outstanding, and all the minimum monthly payments (she only paid the minimum monthly payments). We listed all her assets, the value of the apartment, and her retirement plan. One thing about some of those teachers is that they have great retirement plans, and my girl here was no exception.

We also listed the finance charges associated with each loan and when they would finally be paid off. It didn't look so bad to me. It looked god-awful to Caryn.

"Look how well you've done," I pointed out. "You've saved 17 percent off the top of your salary every year. You have in excess of $150,000 saved for your retirement."

She wasn't moved. "Big deal. I can't retire for nineteen years—how am I supposed to live like a normal human being until then? It's a sad thing when you're in your mid-thirties and all you have to look forward to is retirement." Isn't that the truth? Living as a drudge waiting for retirement for the next nineteen years is not an attractive image.

"I agree," I said, "but I think there is an opportunity here. Do you have loan provisions to borrow from your pension or deferred annuity?"

"Sure I do. But I don't want to borrow."

Now, the interesting thing about people who use their credit cards is that they don't consider it borrowing. They just think of it as owing. That is a very interesting distinction. Somehow the mind thinks of taking a lump sum of money as borrowing, taking a loan as borrowing—but not using credit cards.

I pushed on. "I understand. However, you already are borrowing. You owe money. It says so on the papers you brought me to look at. Let's just figure out how to make this work for you. Are you open to moving the amount you owe around?

"If you pay consumer credit to a credit card company, there is no tax advantage. You don't get a tax deduction for consumer debt interest paid, and the average rate that you are paying is 13.90 percent annually. That means that for every $10,000 you owe—which is just about what you do owe—you pay $1,390 in charges each year to the credit card company. Because you are always carrying a balance, the interest is always accruing; it's called a **rolling balance.** This erodes your ability to save, and because you are paying the minimum monthly payments, almost all of your payment goes toward the charges and little toward the principal."

"I really understand that; that's why I'm here." She wasn't smiling yet.

"Now, if we were to arrange for you to borrow from your pension plan, what rate do you have to pay back at?"

"Seven percent, I think."

"So, if you can follow me for a minute . . . You'll borrow at a lower rate, which cuts your annual cost of borrowing in half, from almost 14 percent to 7 percent. That's the first benefit. The second benefit is that you'll be paying back the interest to yourself. Although you won't feel it now, the money will come back to you in the future."

She brightened. "Also, I can have it deducted directly from my paycheck." The shift in her energy was noticeable.

"Because you'll be reducing your monthly payments by about one-half if you consolidate, you have more cash flow. By that I mean that you will not be paying the other 7 percent in interest. Your interest charges drop about $690 a year, or close to $58 a month."

From Caryn came not exactly a full grin, but a cautious, hopeful smile.

I went on. "I noticed that you get big refunds every year."

"I do get big refunds; that's how I go on vacation."

"Well, that's also how you give the government interest-free loans every year. You can take that same amount difference every pay period and earn interest in a bank."

I call this the old *Christmas club syndrome*. When I was a kid we would bring money to the bank and have them save our money for us. The bank charged no fees, but neither did they pay interest. Just before the holidays, we got our own money back in one check and felt like we'd been given a gift. Better to have banked the money and earned interest. Caryn was having the federal government act as her Christmas club.

Things were starting to get exciting.

"I can call my accountant," she said. "I'll ask how many deductions I should take so that I don't have too much extra taken out of my check. If I do the things that we've been talking about, and I use my tutoring money to pay down the loan faster, I should be almost debt-free soon. I may even buy some new clothing with the increase in my cash flow."

We spent another half hour going over what steps Caryn would be taking. She would pay off her car debt, her credit card debt, and her student loan with one consolidated loan that she would take from her pension. She would arrange for the payments for this loan to be made directly from her paycheck. The money would never come to her—the old out-of-sight, out-of-mind theory. Next, she would apply for a new credit card that offers lower rates for borrowing. She was excited, and animated. Her posture had shifted. She was sitting tall and her voice was strong. We had done very little and yet we had done everything together. She still had the same amount of debts, the same retirement fund, the same income, but a different cash flow—and that made all the difference to Caryn.

The Sandwich Generation

Feeling squeezed, lots of pressure? Don't know which way to turn? Bills got you, kids got you, parents need your help these days? You're part of the Sandwich Generation.

How did they do it? Doesn't it seem like our parents had life simpler? In my world it sure did. Many of us had moms who stayed home and took care of families. Some had moms who worked but it never looked as if they were as confused and pushed and pulled every which way, did it? Maybe they were, but through our eyes they looked able to handle most things well.

Part of what we saw was simplicity. In fact our parents had fewer choices than we have, and that very simplicity created a structure they built their lives around. There was less movement from one home to another, one job to another, one city to another, and one spouse to another. There was a rhythm to the days and weeks of their lives. There were expectations of how things were going to be. These are the parents of the baby boomers I'm talking about. I'm not saying that they were happier or that things were easier, either—just clearer.

Now the baby boomers, those of us approaching 50, are very different from our mothers, and my sense is that we have an entirely different take on life. For that matter, life has a very different take on us.

When I was growing up, my grandmother said she was glad she was as old as she was. She said, "In my day every day was hard but the same hard. Young people have lives that move and change so quickly, and they face dealing with different things all the time. They don't get the peace that I had. When I married your grandfather I knew that I would live in a neighborhood with the same people, watch my children grow, belong to the same clubs; everyone would go to the same schools and Papa would work in the same job always. Now nobody is sure of anything." Boy, was she right.

What I notice more and more as I talk to friends and clients is that they seem to want back some of what they think went on in those days. Of course we tend to romanticize those days, but recent studies and reports tell us that our children may be the first generation not to be able to surpass the generation before them. Your children probably won't be as well-off as you, much less better off. What's happening to the American Dream? Aren't we more educated; don't we work just as hard—maybe harder?

Part of the problem is that the dollar buys less than it used to. Inflation and taxes eat at our paychecks even before we have a chance to spend them. This generation has experienced a decline of buying power. We may make more dollars, but our dollars are buying us less. And the cost of education is inflating at a higher pace than standard inflation. While the historical rate of inflation reported to us by the government is just around 4 percent annually, the rate of inflation for the cost of education is between 7 and 10 percent.

Did you have children when you were in your thirties or even forties? There are plenty of families out there with young children and somewhat older parents. So where previous generations would have been finished with raising the kids and now seriously planning for retirement, many of us are looking at paying college tuition and potentially reduced income at the same time. Unsettling, isn't it? What's more, since we are all living longer—and in fact that is a lovely thought—having older parents can and often does bring its own real concerns. Many of us are finding we are the person who gets to be the filling for the kids-on-one-side, parents-on-the-other sandwich.

Marilyn, a legal secretary, retired about a year ago with a "package," as it's known these days—meaning you take early retirement, you get paid one or more years' salary up front in a lump sum, and you get to keep some benefits like health insurance for a negotiated period of time. Her firm merged with another law firm and she was given an opportunity to take early retirement or risk being laid off in the future with no package. Some choice. At first she was resentful. After all, she had just turned 52. That was thirteen years younger than the age when she had planned to stop working. She was too young to retire, but maybe too old to get hired by a new firm. Now Marilyn is nervous. She was planning on these years to accumulate wealth. Now she has another six months of money left and no real prospects for work. Unemployment will run out soon too, and then what?

Marilyn has been divorced for about seven years now. She and her ex-husband waited until their last child was going away to college so they wouldn't spoil things for the kids. Getting divorced wasn't as bad as she had feared. The marriage had been over for so long that when they finally moved out of the house to their respective new homes it wasn't painful for her at all. It actually felt exciting. Scary, but exciting. She rented a nice two-bedroom apartment in a complex with a lot of other single people. Parking had easy access. There was a security guard at the entrance gate. Her living-room window faced the man-made pond. It was nice to look out at the water when she drank her morning coffee. She bought a sleeper couch for her living room so her kids had their own bed ready and waiting. So, even in that smaller space, the whole family could visit and be together. She wanted them to know that they would always have a home with her.

Marilyn had been working for many years, ever since her younger daughter had gone into first grade. She had seniority in a well-established law firm. This position had been her first job and she had never left. Why leave? She was happy at the firm. Marilyn knew everyone who worked there, all the partners, the legal staff. They were very fond of her. Her office was only a thirty-minute drive from her home. When she started hearing rumors that there might be a merger with another firm, she was concerned about some of her coworkers' losing their jobs, but not herself. She had been with Gil, her boss, for fifteen years. He had seniority, he was a full partner in the firm, so she assumed she was protected. She did wonder if she would have to take on any additional work. Now was not a good time for her to have to worry about that. Her mother was getting very frail and she and her brother had been alternating visits just to keep an eye on her. The visiting nurse stopped by daily and a woman brought over food and cooked, but Marilyn and her brother worried that before long their mother would have to live with one of them or they would have to find alternative care for her. They had been discussing their alternatives. Would she be eligible for a health-related facility, or would she need a nursing home? They had no idea what the process was to find out about these things. They really needed to speak with a social worker.

Marilyn's daughter Sheila was getting married in six months and there was a wedding to plan. Her other daughter, Barbara, had had her first baby only months before. She and her husband were graduate students at the local university and Marilyn baby-sat two nights a week.

Marilyn had planned out her life and set her course for clear sailing right after her divorce. She had met with a financial adviser and created a time line for herself and where she wanted to be at retirement at age 65. The small pension she would get from her employers would not carry her very far, so she had planned ahead. She had invested her money in mutual funds, selecting several funds to create a well-diversified portfolio. The greatest portion of her money was in common stock funds. She had selected an aggressive growth fund, which invests in small companies and new industries, for 10 percent of her money, and growth and income funds, which invest in quality companies that pay consistent dividends and have growth possibilities, with 50 percent of her investment money. The balance of her investment money was in an intermediate-term tax-free mutual bond fund, which invested in municipal bonds. These bonds had less than ten-year maturities and paid tax-free income. In the future she could take the monthly income; for now she was reinvesting it. She had bought an intermediate bond fund because it has less volatility than bonds with longer maturities. She learned that the longer the maturity of a bond the higher the yield but she was willing to forgo higher rate for less risk. Because she was concerned about taxes she chose a municipal bond fund. Municipal bond funds are exempt from federal taxes and if the bonds are from the state you live in they are exempt from state and local taxes too. This was just what she needed.

The stock portion of Marilyn's mutual fund portfolio had been set up with a dividend reinvestment program too. Each time she received dividends or capital gains from the mutual funds she owned, she instructed the mutual fund company to buy more shares for her. She knew that she needed growth in her investments to keep up with inflation. She didn't want to worry about having money to take care of her needs and she was diligent about reaching her goals.

Marilyn and her adviser had built a solid plan, and she was doing well—but not well enough for her to retire now. Not before she was eligible for Social Security, and that wasn't until at least age 62.

She decided to work as a temp for a while. That would help in the short term.

Between worrying about her kids and her mother she felt squeezed and helpless. Her mother's condition was getting worse. The doctors told Marilyn and her brother that there was no way she could be in her home without assistance twenty-four hours a day.

It's too bad that Marilyn's mother didn't have a **long-term-care policy.** Until recent years, nobody thought in those terms. As of now, *44 percent of all Americans age 65 or older are spending at least some time in a nursing home.* Long-term-care policies aren't the answer to all problems; they certainly have their limitations. But they help. Long-term-care policies provide money to offset care at home or in nursing homes. Marilyn's mother could have gotten $80, $100, or more a day toward care. Marilyn decided to look into it for herself when things began to straighten out for her.

Marilyn's mom, Mrs. Broder, wasn't a rich woman, but over the years she and her husband had bought stock and municipal bonds and built a nest egg. Now those monies would be used for her care. There was so much to think about. There were all the Medicare papers to fill out, and the nursing homes to visit so that a nice one could be chosen for her. And, the family worried about what would happen after the money ran out. The social worker affiliated with a local nursing home explained that the children were not responsible for their mother's care and they could apply for Medicaid when funds were no longer available. That was bittersweet news.

Marilyn was becoming an expert on Medicare and Medicaid law. She was an authority on the differences between nursing home care and health-related facilities. She contacted some lawyers in town who were giving classes about elder law and started taking a course one night a week. And that's where she met her new employer. That's right: her new boss is a woman who practices law specializing in issues related to older people.

Marilyn's mother is now in a nursing home. Marilyn visits her mother three times a week at the home, which is only ten minutes from Marilyn's house. She's also joined a support group for care-givers. And her daughters have been wonderful. Barbara visits

Grandma with the baby, and Sheila and her husband stop in for plenty of surprise visits and with stories to share.

Where are the good old times? Were there ever really good old times the way that we want to remember them? Actually, these times aren't too bad; they're just different. But we're different. I'm not interested in washing clothing by hand or giving up my air-conditioning. Come to think of it, when my grandmother lived with us, after my brother and I were out of the house my mother went back to work. It was hard for her to deal with Bubbie all the time. Maybe things aren't that different after all!

Better Than a Good Cleaning Woman

Ever try to find a good baby-sitter or pet-sitter or some-one to clean your house? They're hard to come by.

One of my colleagues tells me the greatest story about her Aunt Ann, which brings this theme to mind . . . and makes me smile.

Ann is 87 years old. Childless, she was widowed about thirty years ago and never remarried. She still lives in the house she and her husband bought over fifty years ago. She used to be a bookkeeper and retired at 65. Since then she's traveled all over the world with friends or by herself on "elder" tours. She stopped driving two years ago; she wasn't happy about giving up the car, but when her car died she figured it was an omen and never bought another one. She uses the bus and takes a taxi in bad weather. She bakes, plays bridge with her friends every week, and makes it to the beauty parlor every Friday for a hairstyling and manicure. She's a pretty feisty woman. She shops at the local store and has everything delivered to her home, where she methodically puts it all away. She doesn't like having anyone help her with this chore because she has a problem with her vision and this way she says she can remember where she puts everything. Her life has been this way for years. Being in her house gives her comfort. She's thought about getting rid of the big old thing, but she feels safe inside those four walls and as long as she can navigate she's going to stay put. She knows every corner and crevice of that place by heart; it holds an awful lot of memories.

Aunt Ann is no stick-in-the-mud; she's always willing to try new and different things. But some kinds of changes, especially one having to do with changing the way she's lived for a long time, make her uncomfortable. I can understand that.

She and her niece Sherry have a very special relationship. She's Sherry's godmother as well as her aunt, and takes her role seriously. When Sherry was little, Ann bought her her first shoes, her first pair of tiny gold earrings, and her first pair of high heels—among many other firsts. She also bought Sherry her first shares of stock and her first savings bonds. When Sherry told her Aunt Ann a secret it remained a secret. She trusted her aunt's opinion, and often asked her for guidance. What she really liked most about Aunt Ann was that once she had said what she thought, she let Sherry make the final decision—unlike Sherry's mom, who could never let go. Ann was five years younger than Sherry's mom, but she seemed a generation younger to Sherry. Ann was a businesswoman. She was exciting and fun to be around. Sherry's mom was great, but she was . . . her mom. Aunt Ann was just the best.

So when Sherry decided to leave teaching and go back to school to become a financial adviser, she went to Aunt Ann's house and talked to her for hours about what it would mean to change her career, what the pluses and minuses were. They talked about the fact that there would be no more guaranteed salary, and thus no more financial security. Basically, Sherry would be starting her own business. There would be no more sick days or vacation days, and only a few holidays, when the stock market closes. They also talked about the fact that Sherry would be an independent businesswoman, her earnings dependent on her ability. She could grow and build, and in fact the sky was the limit. Ann thought Sherry could do anything. Maybe she was a little biased, but she really thought that Sherry had everything to make it in the business world. She had integrity, a great personality, brains, and a strong work ethic. Sherry always appreciated her aunt's love and support. She says she will always remember how important it was to have Aunt Ann rooting for her during those days that she was struggling with her career decision.

That was twenty-five years ago. Aunt Ann was right: Sherry turned out to be a successful and well-respected financial adviser. When she first started out, her aunt would come to the office to help out. She would file, sort, and get things ready to mail. She did whatever was needed and it gave her great pleasure to assist.

Even today she still cuts out articles she thinks Sherry might find interesting or useful for her business. For example, recently she found a magazine article about the value of creating **living trusts** for older people. Of course, she sent it out to Sherry with a loving note and called to ask her if she would mind coming over for a business visit. When the two women sat down at the kitchen table to have their coffee, they began to talk about the article on trusts.

"I know that I have been really resistant to changing anything that your uncle and I set up, but that article made me start thinking," Aunt Ann said. "I know you've mentioned setting up a living trust many times. I guess I just wasn't open to the idea, but I think I'm ready now. After all, Sherry, I may have only ten good years left. I want to feel secure that everything is in order in case I get sick. I also don't want to create a burden for you. The article said that we could put everything I own into a trust, and as long as I'm in shape I can make all the decisions about my finances. I could name you as the other trustee on the trust, besides myself. That way if anything did happen where I was sick or incapacitated, you could automatically be the person who already had access to everything in the trust and handle things. The trust could not only spell out who makes the decisions about my money but it could also give you permission to make my medical decisions for me. Do you mind being the other trustee on my trust, dear?"

"Of course I don't mind," Sherry answered without hesitating. "I love you. I'd just like to clarify some things about all of this information that you read and sent me a copy of. And of course, we'll need to pay a visit to a lawyer.

"The trust that you are talking about is also known as an **inter vivos trust,**" Sherry explained. "You are correct when you say that you can be the trustee of your own trust, Aunt Ann. When you pass on, the trust will already have been set up to transfer everything as you have directed. Because your assets will be in a trust, they will avoid probate. But remember, that does not mean they will avoid estate taxes. **Probate** is a legal process that makes sure your will is valid and allows the person you've named in your will as executor or executrix to make sure your last wishes are carried out.

"You still will need to create a **durable power of attorney** if you want me to make medical decisions for you if you are incapacitated It is sometimes known as a **health care proxy.** The trust does not cover that issue. Also, Aunt Ann, if you have specific wishes about artificially maintaining life support should you become terminally ill, you may want to create a **living will** as well. A living will is used to make clear and specific what your wishes are if you become unable to speak for yourself—for example, if you do not want any life-sustaining treatments used."

Sherry was glad that her aunt had thought about these issues. It would help her as well as her aunt if a trust, a durable power of attorney, and a living will were created.

Aunt Ann had some further thoughts. "I'd like to give some money away to charity now while I'm here to see them enjoy it. I can give away unlimited amounts to charity in my lifetime and not have to worry about paying any taxes. There are no taxes on charitable giving. I won't use up my money playing bridge and taking my small trips. There is no mortgage on this house—it's all paid up—and I manage very well on my Social Security and income from our investments. I think I'm going to make some donations to my favorite causes. That way I can get to see the money put to work while I'm still around. That's a nice idea.

"For that matter, I don't even have to worry about your having to pay estate taxes either. My accountant, Terry, told me that the federal government allows me to leave $600,000 to other people at the time of my death without them having to pay estate taxes. I don't have $600,000 in what will be my estate when I'm gone anyway. I guess I have no problem there at all—well, actually *you* won't have the problem; I'll be gone. You'll just have to pay whatever state taxes there are. I didn't know that each state has their own state taxes; I thought it was just the federal government that collected money when someone dies. You will only have to pay the state when I die. When your uncle and I did our planning years ago we never thought about these things. Can you imagine me being so fancy to talk about living trusts and estate taxes!"

Aunt Ann is a very generous lady. Every year she gives Sherry and her brother Tom each $10,000 as a gift. That was one of the ways she was able to keep her future estate from being over $600,000. Giving away the money meant it did not continue to be in her name and did not appreciate in value by accumulating interest or by capital appreciation. If you give $10,000 or less to someone—it can be anyone; these gifts are not limited to family—you are not required to declare it to the government. It is not applied to your lifetime estate exemption of $600,000. You can give these gifts away to as many people as you want as long as they are $10,000 or less in a calendar year to each person. These gifts are not taxable to the person who receives them, either. What a deal!

Sherry made an appointment to have an attorney friend of hers talk to them about setting up a trust and redoing Aunt Ann's will. The following Thursday the two of them went into town, to put the wheels in motion with the attorney. Afterward, the two women talked over lunch.

"I know that this is no big deal to you," Aunt Ann told Sherry, "because you deal with these issues all the time. But it makes me feel safe to know we have all our ducks in a row here. I will be able to sleep better at night knowing that things are neat and proper. As soon as the papers are all signed and done, I can go on vacation with a clear mind. You know, Sherry, it's great having you. Having people to take care of me, like you and your attorney friend, is a real relief. It's almost as good as finding a good cleaning woman."

Something to Remember Me By

It was Mother's Day. My Aunt Ellen and I were going out to eat Chinese food on Kings Highway. She had turned 80 that year. Neither of us have our kids living near enough to visit. Both of us are single—she's a widow, I'm divorced. We get along well and have had some great times telling stories and just hanging out. I like to think of her as ageless. I like to think that she'll always be around.

I took the D train to her house that day and met her right near the train station. She still lives in Flatbush, the neighborhood I grew up in. I like to walk around there. Even though the stores have changed and the people look different, being there still makes me feel warm and fuzzy inside. I had some wonderful days on the streets near Kings Highway.

We walked arm in arm, my Aunt Ellen and I, toward Coney Island Avenue and the Chinese restaurant. It's the same place where we had held my Uncle Mitty's eightieth birthday party. Mitty, Ellen's husband, died suddenly about ten years ago. He had the flu and just died. My aunt says she's sorry she didn't remarry; it's very lonely for her without having another person to be with. Actually they fought all the years they were together, but still it was their marriage; it was the way of living that she knew. She hadn't known any other way for almost fifty years.

As we walked along chatting, she directed me toward the entrance of a jewelry store. "I want to go in, and don't argue with me," she said. "I want to buy you something to leave you, for when I'm dead."

"What are you talking about?"

"Look, I love you and I don't have a lot of things. You're my special niece. Now I want to start handling things for the future. When I die, my grandchildren will get what little jewelry I have left, and I want you to have something to remember me by. Don't argue with me! I want to get you something that you like in the jewelry store now."

"It's Mother's Day and the prices will be sky high. We'll come back another day."

"No, we won't—I made up my mind, we're gonna do it today, right now while I have you here, while we're together and I'm still healthy. I have my credit card with me. Don't hurt my feelings."

We walked into the jeweler's hand in hand. The counter woman looked up. "Can I help you?"

"This is my dear niece," said Aunt Ellen. "I want to buy something for her to have when I die."

The saleswoman looked uncomfortable and I couldn't help but smile. "She's not dying now," I said to comfort this stranger.

"I'm just getting things ready—after all, I'm not a baby. Look at me. How old do you think I am?" said my aunt.

Poor saleslady. "Sixty-five?"

"Don't be ridiculous. I'll be eighty in a few weeks . . . and it's a milestone. I have to be responsible. I've got to get things ready. You know what I mean?"

The nice lady nodded. This was Kings Highway, home of more than a few Golden Age groups and lots of AARP members. She was just uncomfortable with my aunt's enthusiasm.

In the meantime, two other salespeople had come over to chat. "That's very nice of you to worry about your niece," said one.

"I'm superstitious—when my parents want to talk to me about dying, I change the conversation. I'll handle things when I have to," said the other. "Doesn't this all feel eerie to you?" she asked me.

"Nonsense," my aunt answered for me. "It's all part of living. Did you ever hear of anyone going on forever? Even my grandmothers—they lived to be old ladies but they died too. Did you ever hear the horror stories that happen when you don't talk to anybody, when nobody knows what's going on in your life? Just like you have to plan to live, you have to plan to die. When you don't let your parents tell you what they need to, that's selfish. They have to finish up their business. Maybe they have final wishes. How would they like to be buried? Maybe they have money you will need to handle, or maybe they have left someone else in charge that you will have to contact. There are plenty of things that you might have to know. I don't have much, but I do know friends of mine who went to lawyers and advisers to do estate planning. What I'm doing now is important."

"They're entitled to get that handled; it's just that it's gory to plan to die," our saleswoman said with a shudder.

But for Aunt Ellen to feel freed up to go on living, she needed to put things in order to die. It was more than making a will, or appointing a medical guardian, although those things were very important too: she needed to put her entire house in order. She's a take-charge lady and she was taking charge, and making people uncomfortable with what she considered to be a very natural order of events. Look at the stir it was causing in the jewelry store. She was enjoying every minute of it.

While they discussed the merits of planning to die, I picked out a pair of small pearl earrings. No doubt they were seriously overpriced, but Aunt Ellen wanted to shop, so we would shop.

"Gift wrap it with a bow," she said. "It's for my wonderful niece. Something to remember me by."

"Cash or charge?"

"Charge. I have insurance on my credit cards too, so if I drop dead my kids don't get stuck with any bills," she said proudly.

"Thanks, and stay well," all the people in the store called out as we left.

"I will," she said. "Happy Mother's Day."

"I don't know what all the to-do is," she said. "You'd think dying is a new concept."

"It's not that," I answered. "Some people just feel that their planning for someone to die moves things along. Or that when they bring up planning, the others will think they're being greedy or selfish."

"Listen, things gotta get handled. When your uncle died everything was upside down. Which brings me to another point. I'd like you to take me over to Coney Island Avenue soon to pick out my coffin. I don't want anybody paying for it. I'm a proud woman."

"Okay, when the weather gets cooler, but you'll have to hang on till then!"

"All right, but don't forget: I want to have everything handled so I can enjoy my life. Now, let's go to the Chinese restaurant. I can't wait to have chow mein. I haven't had it in weeks."

Thanks, Aunt Rose

Wouldn't it be nice if some long-lost relative that you knew, or maybe never knew at all, remembered you in their will? What would you do? What would life be like?

Alex is a cabdriver. Driving cabs has always been his work; he likes it because he can meet interesting people that way and he has control of his own destiny. He determines the shifts he drives and the days he works. No holidays or weekends, that's for sure. He feels like a free agent and that makes him happy. Sure there's stress, but what job doesn't have stress? He bought his taxi in 1960. His wife Holly and he live in a small two-family house that they bought when he got out of the army after the war in Korea. He was able to get a mortgage under the GI bill. Holly is a secretary for one of the businesses in their town. She's been working there for over twenty years. Her boss often travels and she runs the show. It's a three-person operation—Holly, her boss, and the bookkeeper. There are no pension benefits, but there is a good medical plan, two weeks' paid vacation, sick time if she needs it, and as long as the business is around she'll always have a job. It's a comfortable life.

Alex and Holly had always talked about saving for retirement, but frankly, there was hardly money left over after they'd paid all their bills and paid for the small vacations that they take each year. They always felt it was their duty as parents to pay for everything for their two girls until they got married. That meant the whole deal—clothing, school, cars, and of course weddings. Thank God the girls each got married right after college graduation. Both weddings were done with great taste and left beautiful memories and some big bills. At least they had paid off their mortgage a few years ago. Now they did have some money to put away from time to time, but the prices of things kept going up faster than their income. So from the looks of things, unless a miracle happened they would always have to work some and never be able to retire completely.

Then came the call from an attorney in Florida. Holly's aunt, her mother's sister Rose, had died, and they were requested to attend the reading of the will.

What in the world did they need to spend the money on an airline ticket for? Couldn't the lawyer just tell them what the will said? "No, your aunt requested that you and your cousins Patrick and Harry be present at the reading. Please speak with them so that you can all be here at the same time and we can get things handled."

So Holly called Pat and Harry and they set a time to fly to Miami and meet at the lawyer's office. Alex decided to join them and make a small vacation with his wife out of the whole thing.

Aunt Rose was way up there in her nineties. Nobody knew exactly how high up, but if you consider that she was the baby in Holly's mother's family and all the other sisters and brothers had been gone for some time and they had lived to very respectable ages, then she had to be right up there. Rose had buried four husbands. After the last one, she had vowed never to marry again, and she had kept that vow. Until then—this was only seven or eight years ago— Rose had never lived for more than one year without being married throughout her adult life. She was the bohemian in the family. She traveled and studied abroad and she was known for the soirees that she had in her home with her artist and writer friends. Each of her husbands was in some way part of the art scene. The children always loved to be around Aunt Rose and whoever she was with at the time. She was so interesting and different.

Despite her great desire to have children, Rose was never blessed with her own, and she liked to think of her niece and nephews as the next best thing. Every year at birthday and holiday time, regardless of where Rose was living and who she was married to, she always remembered her Holly, Patrick, and Harry. Every present from her had some little note attached explaining where it had been purchased and some enchanting story explaining its special meaning. Rose had very little money. Money wasn't her thing; it was too capitalistic to have money, and Rose was a socialist. But she never failed to remember the children with something special.

As the years passed and Holly, Patrick, and Harry grew up, Aunt Rose remembered the children with notes and gifts. Even though she had moved to Miami from New York and didn't get to see them, she never forgot. Holly had visited her just a few years ago in her small one-bedroom apartment right near the beach. Rose loved it there. The neighborhood wasn't the same as when she had moved there, but she loved it just the same. She loved the ocean and the beach. They took a long walk there every afternoon during the visit they had together. Holly wanted Rose to consider going into a nursing home because she was suffering from high blood pressure and bouts of dizzy spells, but Rose would hear nothing of it. Maybe Rose would consider having someone help her by cleaning once a week. There were old newspapers and books strewn everywhere. "No way," said Rose. "I have no money to waste on that."

Aunt Rose died in her sleep one night. Her neighbor hadn't heard from her all day and called the police because she was getting worried—it just wasn't like Rose to not stop by. Rose was gone! The family was called. They flew Rose's body home to have the funeral. It's very expensive to fly a body in a coffin, but the children decided that they would like to give that to Aunt Rose as a final gift. They all chipped in. She would be buried in the family plot next to her husbands. After all, she had been fond of each and every one.

That's why it seemed somewhat ridiculous to go back to Miami. They could have just had someone come in to scrub the place and put together the furnishings for the Salvation Army to pick up. Oh well, Holly would go over to the apartment and see if there were any mementos to take home after her visit with the lawyer. It seemed funny that Aunt Rose would even have a will.

The lawyer was a very nice man. He invited the four of them to sit down and offered them coffee. Everyone declined—Patrick and Harry were in a rush; they had to make a plane back the same day. It was only Holly and Alex that were staying.

"I will read the will, then," the lawyer said. "Your Aunt Rose was insistent that you all be together."

And then he read, and the more he read the wider everyone's eyes became and the more their mouths hung open. Aunt Rose had real estate holdings. Not only did she own the apartment that she was living in (apparently she had purchased it while she was married to her third husband), she also had a stock and bond portfolio and, according to the papers that were read, jewelry that was kept in a safe deposit box in the local bank. Could this be our dear sweet socialist Aunt Rose? Indeed it was! And by the looks of things, the old girl had been quite an investor at that. Who would have had believed it?

Everything was left to her niece and nephews equally. There was more than $1 million—no kidding.

Even after paying all the estate taxes on the $400,000 in excess of what she could pass on estate-tax-free, there was plenty left. Bonanza!! They were speechless. The lawyer would give them all the details to take home and review and they could decide how they would dispose of the assets. They could advise him accordingly later. He would take care of all of the legal matters. *Estate taxes were due within nine months of death.* CONGRATULATIONS!

Holly and Alex drove Pat and Harry to the airport. They went on to Aunt Rose's place and started to put things together for charity collection. Lord, that place was a mess. She certainly could have had help if she had chosen to. They found passbooks from eight different local banks while they were looking through the desk. Each one was set up in trust for one of the grandnieces and grandnephews. They found EE savings bonds that had been accumulated over the last thirty-five or so years. These things weren't even mentioned by the lawyer and, no kidding, they found an envelope with cash—more than $2,000—marked "Emergency Money" in the freezer. Good thing that they hadn't hired a cleaning service to defrost the refrigerator.

Within months the estate was settled. Alex and Holly had decided to move to Florida and relocate. They weren't ready to retire completely, but thanks to Aunt Rose they could afford to start over in a new place with peace of mind. They would come north to visit their children three or four times a year. What a wonderful gift she had left them. They still couldn't get over the mystery about Aunt Rose and her money. What had made her do the things she did?

When the final letter came from the lawyer it was accompanied by a handwritten note from Aunt Rose:

My Dear Children,

I hope this note finds you all well. Please accept the gifts left to you with my love and good wishes. Over the years, I accumulated this wealth piece by piece. It never seemed to be much at the time, but I put away a little as I had it. I never cared much about money; it was just a vehicle to get to do the other things that I wanted to do in my life. The only thing that I worried about was being a burden in my old age. Since I had no children to take care of me, I was concerned about the later days of my life. It happens that I was a very lucky woman because I had my husbands that loved me, great friends, and my health. I lived the way I wanted to. Because I saved for a rainy day I always felt secure. I had everything that I wanted and never wanted to live any way other than I did. It was enough for me just to know that the money was there. Please feel free to use the gifts that I have left you as you see fit in any way that it makes you happy. The only regret I have is that I will not be able to see you have the pleasure in using it. Perhaps I should have shared some of it while I was alive, but that would have blown my image of being the socialist, free spirit Rose and I enjoyed that image. I never wanted you to know that there was another side of me—Responsible, Rainy Day Rose.

So there it is. Bless you all and enjoy life to its fullest!

With much love,
Aunt Rose

Next to the place that Alex and Holly built they have hung a small sign: CHEZ ROSE.

Dorothy . . . You Are the Wizard!

Of course you remember Dorothy and the story of *The Wizard of Oz*? So you must remember that Oz is not a place on the map and that in the end Dorothy finds that all along she had what she needed to make her life what she wanted it to be!

She was a very nice girl who wasn't satisfied with the way her life was going and started out on an adventure that changed her entire outlook. When she started out she was looking for the wizard to give her the answers that would enable her to turn things around. In the end, of course, she discovered *she* was the wizard. You should take a lesson from Dorothy.

Plenty of us have hoped to find that special someone who will give us the answers. Hoping and wishing that we could just turn over things to someone else, we keep searching for that other person who will know everything. I used to be that way myself. Some of you are still waiting for someone else to be your wizard, to make you feel safe and taken care of, when *you have* everything you will ever need yourself. Getting help is fine but giving up the driver's seat is another thing altogether.

When you are in charge, you know that *you have the ability to make decisions, take action, and get results.* That's a mighty powerful package to be the owner of. If you keep thinking that the answers lie outside of you, then you can never be secure; you are always questioning your own wisdom and ability. When you rely on the wizard that lives outside of you, and if things work when you haven't been involved with the decision making, you are happy but you feel that you really can't be sure of your ability to manage things yourself. If, on the other hand, you are open to the possibility that the wizard's address is at your house, that the wisdom you seek is within you, then you'll find, as Dorothy found out, that *you* have the ability to get all the answers to all your questions. As you may have noticed, I keep trying to point out that *it's always up to you!* But don't get confused: I'm not saying to go it alone. Get all the assistance that you need— but even that is *your choice.* You are the chooser, you are the wizard.

Carolyn is a widow. Her husband John was an accountant and an attorney. She was a housewife from the beginning of their marriage, in 1960, until he died. They had two sons and enjoyed a comfortable family life. John made partner in his firm while Carolyn took care of the children and did charity work for the homeless shelter in her community and her church. They took family vacations together with the kids and vacations alone for the two of them. Except during tax season, they all ate dinner together just about every night. He handled the money, she handled the kids. He filled out the tax return, she signed it. He talked to the insurance man, she approved the purchases. He selected the stocks and bonds to buy, she said okay. She never questioned John's decisions. She never read the statements when they came from the bank or brokerage firm. She could have if she wanted to; she just didn't want to. After all, she had her jobs and he had his.

The kids grew up and moved out; the parents were still young. They had a lot of living left to do and they planned on doing it all. They were going to travel and play golf. Their house in Connecticut had a small mortgage left. They were planning on eventually buying a house in a retirement community somewhere with a warmer cli- mate, like Florida or Arizona. That was down the road a ways, but for now John was in good shape and he planned on working at least another five to seven years.

Everyone in the family looked up to John—he was the wizard, the guy you could always count on. He took care of any legal or tax problems for anyone in the family. John just took care of things for everybody in general. He guided his neighbors and friends. He was a great family man and he cared about everybody. There was no reason to worry when he was in charge.

Then the wizard dropped dead, right in the front garden while he was raking the leaves. Carolyn found him lying there and thought he was playing a joke on her. John was always playing jokes. But John never got up. That was two years ago.

When John died everything happened so fast. He died on Saturday and was buried on Monday. The sons came home and helped their mother make funeral arrangements. Carolyn walked through the entire experience in a dream state. The neighbors pitched in. The family stayed together. Friends dropped by to see what they could do. There was nothing to do.

The insurance man called after he heard of John's death to give his condolences. He wanted to go over the papers that Carolyn would need to sign, so he made an appointment for the following week. John's partners at the law firm said that they would like to be of service in any way possible. She knew what was in the will. There was nothing to rush about; everything had been left to her. John had set up the will himself. There was enough money in their joint checking account to pay whatever bills needed to be paid for now.

Then the sons went back to their respective homes, the neighbors and friends to their business at hand, and Carolyn was alone.

At first Carolyn kept busy doing all kinds of things. Work at the shelter took care of her time two days a week; she gardened; she visited with neighbors. Then she went to hear the reading of the will. Her sons stayed only a couple of days this time; they had commitments to get back to. As she had expected, John had set up the will to make life simple: everything was left to Carolyn.

She asked the lawyer if there would be any problems legally if she postponed all the "business" she would have to take care of because of John's death. When they explained that there was nothing that had to be handled immediately, she was relieved. She couldn't think about the future just yet. It took all her energy to live day to day. She had lunch with friends, and she made lots of trips to visit friends and relatives out of town. John had always said that she would need to supplement her income if something happened to him. So she followed his instructions right away and got a part-time job as an assistant in a small real estate office in town. The law firm where John had been a partner continued to pay his salary for the three months after he died, until year's end. She made a decision to do nothing about getting his name off the credit cards, the car insurance, and the house. She would leave his name on everything for now. Dealing with the name changes at the bank and brokerage house where they had their accounts was too difficult emotionally, too final. It was all too soon; she knew she would have to deal with all these issues later, but that took work and she was feeling very emotional. She would just pay the bills for now, and handle everything else in due time.

Around the first of the year Carolyn made the decision to move from her home in northern Connecticut to New York City. Her kids were gone, John was gone, and she was thinking about what she, Carolyn, wanted to do. Her mind was whirring and spinning. There were days when she felt like a kid, with so many choices and such excitement awaiting her. Then there were the other days when the road looked bleak and empty and she was angry and fearful. John had left her with maps on how to get to Cape Cod, lists on taking care of the furnace and when to change the air filters, instructions on who to call if the computer stopped working, and of course who to call in an emergency if he wasn't around. He had always made lists for when he was away on business trips. He had been great about all of that; but she had depended on him for so much more. She needed her wizard back and she couldn't have him. So she would just have to set off to find a new wizard. This required a new beginning. She had a hell of a ride ahead of her. How could he have left her? He broke his promise to be around forever. This just wasn't the way things were supposed to have gone.

She took a trip to New York. It was exhausting. She didn't know the subways or the buses, or even that you couldn't hail a taxi unless the light was on on top of the cab. The first time she went out to eat alone in a restaurant, she sat down and wept bitter tears in public.

She stayed in a small midtown hotel, accessible to everywhere easily. The next day she made appointments with a local realtor so she could get a feel for the neighborhoods she might want to live in. Her head was so foggy at the end of the day that she ordered room service—an extravagance for a widow on a limited income, she realized, but she went for it anyway. Her body ached and her bed felt like the safest place she could be. But the next morning she was off again. Carolyn liked Gramercy Park; she also liked Greenwich Village. God, how she wished John were there to make the decision; he would know which location would be best for them as an investment. But he wasn't there, and now it was about what *she* liked best, and she'd just have to do some research. After all, she was a smart woman. This was not the end of the world, it just felt like it. She thanked the real estate brokers, got her train ticket, and went back to Connecticut.

Carolyn called her friend Ellyn, who had worked for years as a broker at the same real estate office as Carolyn. Ellyn explained that if Carolyn was buying a co-op she needed to review the **black book** or **offering prospectus,** which would give her plenty of information about the building, the financial status of the corporation that was set up by the shareholders of the building, and the other rules and regulations she would have to follow as an owner. She also gave her a list of questions to ask. The words Ellyn spoke sounded like a foreign language. When Carolyn called to speak with the brokers in Manhattan, she apologized for being stupid. "I'm sorry, I've never done this before and I'm not even sure about what I'm asking or if I'm asking this right." They understood her completely and were more than happy to help. After all, they also knew that Carolyn would be making the decision and writing the check.

She decided to buy a one-bedroom apartment in Greenwich Village, off Charles Street, in a building with a doorman and an elevator. She didn't want to walk up stairs anymore. She had carried laundry up from the basement to the bedrooms for years. Enough lifting and pulling. If she had to choose for herself, then she would, and she'd get just what she wanted. There was a small park on the next corner where she could sit on sunny days if she wanted to, and a big Sloan's supermarket down the street that delivered food orders. She had enough money to buy the apartment outright. Rather than apply for a mortgage, she would use the proceeds from the sale of her current home to pay for the new place. That way she would have to concern herself only with the monthly maintenance charge, which Carolyn felt would be doable.

"Doable" was becoming a whole new concept. She was going to sell both her cars and move to the big city. She would take subways or buses during the days and taxis or car service at night. She put her house on the market the same day that she decided to buy her co-op and listed it with her current employers. The house was priced right and sold within a month. Things were certainly on the move. The neighbors talked behind her back for a while—after all, where did she think she was going at her age of fifty four? Carolyn and Ellyn thought that some of them might have been jealous that she had the courage to start out for herself. Her children supported her decision to "go for it." They helped her pack and had a garage sale. That morning was pretty awful for the boys, and worse for Carolyn. The contents of a lifetime together marked down for resale, no longer of any value to the remaining spouse and children. As the people came by to pick through and bargain, Carolyn and her sons laughed and shared stories with each other about what John would think of all of this. They made $850 that day.

She met with the cooperative board where she was buying her apartment. It felt a little like joining a college sorority. They made her provide financial information about how much money she had and where it was invested. Her accountant prepared the financial state-ment for her to give to the board. They also required a couple of years' tax returns. What would that tell them? The returns were based on when John was alive. She wasn't sure what she was supposed to do or say at the meeting, but apparently she did it well and said it well, because she was approved.

She asked the real estate broker who she should call for home-owner's insurance and ordered insurance for theft, water damage, and fire. She was starting to feel a degree of confidence. She sold and bought both homes within twenty-four hours. A partner from John's firm handled the closing in Connecticut; a new lawyer in Manhattan referred by her younger son took care of the Charles Street place. She thought, How could you have done this to me, damn you, John, and then the moving van came.

In New York Carolyn opened a checking account at a local bank. They asked her for her credit references and she had none. Every-thing had John's Social Security number on it. They muddled through that problem, although the way the people at the bank acted you would have thought they had never worked with a widow before. Lord knows there are lots of Carolyns running around. She was so put off she demanded to talk to the branch manager. The branch manager apologized and took care of Carolyn personally. She also suggested that Carolyn put the credit cards into her name rather than keeping them in John's. Until now the cards had been issued with him as the primary owner, based on his ability to pay, and she had been issued a card as his wife.

Back at her new apartment she called the credit card companies and explained her plight. Yes, they said, *it was true she was working part-time and could afford to pay her bills,* but if they took John's name off she would have to expect to lower her credit line when she reapplied under her own Social Security number. Her income was less than his. Were they kidding? Why would they lower the amount she could charge, when she had been responsible about the bills all these years?

"I applied for the card and paid the bills all the years that both my husband and I used those bloody cards! My husband told me that was just as good as having a card in my own name."

"Well, he was wrong, lady," was the reply. "How would you like to handle this?"

So Carolyn accepted the new card with her name but under John's credit line, with a commitment to apply elsewhere for her own credit with another credit card company. She would have to start the process from the beginning: as just plain "Carolyn," not "Mrs. John," filling out applications and building up credit for herself. Maybe she'd start with American Express or an individual store. This time everything would be in her name and under her Social Security number. How was it possible to assign a higher credit rating to a dead man than to his widow?

Carolyn took a job at a law firm in the city, working daily from 3 to 11 P.M. doing data entry, in order to have the extra money that John had told her to plan for. She made $7 an hour, without benefits. That was another thing: her insurance coverage under COBRA, the law that allows you to maintain health insurance coverage generally for up to eighteen months after loss of a job or death of a spouse, was almost up—she had learned that from the personnel department at John's old firm—and she had to get new coverage. Another thing she had never been taught about. She hadn't planned on the fact that once John died she wouldn't be eligible to participate in his plan for longer than eighteen months. Dear God!

The insurance representative kept calling her to set up an appointment to discuss what she wanted to do with the money that had been left to her from John's life insurance policy. She didn't want to talk yet. She had to deal with one thing at a time. She felt that the monies could stay in a money market account earning interest until she had a clearer picture of what she needed to be doing. Making a rash decision could be costly in the long run; best hold on. Death, Divorce and Disaster are hard times to try to make changes. She took one step at a time. First she changed the names on all her bank and brokerage accounts. Next she started to think about how she would feel most comfortable investing her money. She was going to understand as much as she could, step by step. She'd read some books, take some classes, and start asking lots of questions. This was *her* money and she wanted to understand about her money.

Carolyn began to make new friends with people who were different from those she had known for years. Maggie, who lived in her new building, was a writer. Howard and Robert, neighbors next door, were both involved in computer programming. Mrs. Lillian Anderson walked her dog and sat in the park every day. That's where she and Carolyn met. Mrs. Anderson was in her eighties, but she and Carolyn had a lot in common. Her husband had died just three years ago.

One afternoon Carolyn and Mrs. Anderson were having tea together and talking about life.

"You're lucky, in a way, that John died early," Mrs. Anderson was saying. "At least you have an opportunity to learn what you need to so that you can feel secure about yourself. I'm learning, but it's hard at this stage to undo some of the things that were done by my husband. After all, *you* can still get long-term care and disability insurance. It's too late for me now. I have to worry about my kids having a burden. You can invest your money so that you can get extra income coming to you if you want, or put it into stocks that will give you the potential for growth. My husband put everything we had into stocks—that's nice if you are younger, but for me there's not enough diversification, not enough income, and I could use some extra income these days. The stocks do pay dividends, but not very much. Some do, you know, like utilities, but not the ones we have. Now the stock has appreciated so much in value because he bought it at so much lower a price. If I were to sell it, I would have to pay a very large amount of long-term capital gains taxes. It will be better if I leave it in my estate to my children and grandchildren. When they inherit the stock, it will pass on to them at the cost price as of the date of my death, not at what was paid for it. But that doesn't help me much. It doesn't give me much income to live on.

"I never dealt with these issues while Mr. Anderson was alive, and now it feels like so much to learn in so little time. I wish I had asked more questions, not only of my husband but of our accountants and lawyers. I'm not even sure that he asked that many questions either;

he just followed their advice. But I ask plenty of questions now. They might not like it so much, but too bad. It's my money and my life and I'm asking until I understand."

Carolyn sympathized. "You know, I've been taking some classes and working with a financial adviser. I thought that John knew everything. I'm finding out that he was just a very kind, smart man, but he wasn't perfect. I think now that he should have set up an **irrevocable life insurance trust** and arranged for the trust to own the insurance on his life. The way he had it, I was named owner and beneficiary. That was meant to be very thoughtful—I know he wanted me to have control of our money, or maybe he thought it wasn't a good idea to set up a trust for other reasons. After all, there are pros and cons to everything. But we should have discussed it.

"I know he never thought of us as being wealthy, but if you add in everything that he left to me, it's way more than $600,000. You see, he could pass unlimited amounts to me at his death because I am his spouse, but the problem arises when I die. The problem is my estate. Anything that I leave over $600,000 will be subject to estate taxes. Our house had appreciated dramatically. We paid only $40,000, but that was years ago. It had gone up in value tenfold. By the way, I'm quitting my job. Now that things have calmed down I find I have more than enough income to live on. Anyway, I understand that we might have been better off with what is known as a **wealth transfer trust.** The trust would have been the owner and the beneficiary of the policy. I could have been a recipient of the trust, getting income, and then the boys would have gotten the principal after my death. The other thing we could have done is purchase a **second to die policy.** The premiums are lower than having two separate policies. It pays the insurance benefit at the time of death of the second spouse—in this case, it will be after my death. That would have helped our children with the estate taxes too. Either of those ideas would have helped to retain everything that we worked so hard for. I'd like to leave something for my boys, and it would have been nice to have John's thoughts on the subject.

"I thought that just because John knew about taxes, he knew about estate planning too, but maybe he didn't. It's *really important* to see an attorney and review estate matters; I see that now. As a matter of fact, I've now bought insurance on my own life so that my kids can handle paying any estate taxes on what they inherit when I go.

That way I can enjoy my money and not worry for the kids. I just had to rewrite my will. Laws change over the years, and John hadn't changed anything ever; so it was a good time to make sure things were in order. You won't believe this, but I also found some old stock certificates in the bureau drawer that are worthless. In my mind, well, I thought he was perfect and knew everything in these matters. It's nice to find out that he was as human as the rest of us.

"Oh well, I was afraid to look at all of this, thinking that I'm not very smart, but I never learned or wanted to learn before. Really, I can't blame John for not knowing everything, or myself for that matter, for not wanting to know. This is not a time for blame. I wanted to live in the dark, and now I've decided to see things more clearly. We had good years together. It makes me feel like I'm becoming an adult. If I survived John's dying, I feel like I'll survive all this. Actually it's even kind of exciting. I'm carving out my own path."

Facts We Learned:

SECURITY

Mutual funds are professionally managed portfolios of stocks and/or bonds, or a mixture of both.

Dollar cost averaging is a system usually used with mutual fund investing which automatically invests fixed amounts of money at predetermined time intervals.

College tuition costs have been rising faster than the rate of inflation.

Each person gets a federal tax credit for the tax that would be due on $600,000 of their estate. Avoiding probate does not mean that you can avoid paying taxes.

Planning should include not only wills but any or all of the following: durable power of attorney, health care proxy, living will, trusts.

Lessons We Learned:

SECURITY

A sense of security is a major component of achieving success.

As your life changes, so will your concept of security, depending on:

> your marital status: single, married, in a committed relationship, divorced, widowed
>
> your employment situation: working, retired, unemployed, changing careers
>
> your financial commitments: children, parents, retirement planning, education planning, health insurance, life insurance, estate planning

You will always be redesigning, modifying, and changing how you view yourself and your needs.

Planning will help you feel secure.

Give yourself permission to change your opinion.

RISK

RISK

1. Areas in my life where I have taken risks are _____.

2. Usually when I take risks the results are _____.

3. I am more apt to take risks if _____.

4. My definition of risk is _____.

5. Taking risks with money means _____.

6. Talking about taking risks makes me _____.

7. If I take risks then I _____.

8. I understand _____ about risks related to investments.

Risk

What are you prepared to lose?
What can go wrong?
What if you do? What if you don't?

There's always risk in each choice
we make—
There's always the chance of
making mistakes.

Risk is part of the process,
it's just part of life.
Don't let it scare you
or cause you strife!

Marriage to Mr. Rosenstein, or
What Price Romance?

Did you know that 50 percent of all marriages end in divorce? Of course you did. Everyone knows the statistics. But did you know that most people don't plan on being part of the 50 percent that fails? That would be a very unromantic notion, wouldn't it?

My grandmother was the first in our family to get divorced.

Bubbie Chasha, the one who moved back into my parents' house when I was 10, had been married twice. I've already told you how she found Papa Sam, my grandfather. He was the man she met through a matchmaker right after she arrived in America as an immigrant. He was the father of her children. He died when I was 2. That made my grandmother a fairly young widow. You may remember that she hadn't worked and had stayed home to be with the family, as most wives did in those times. It's not that they could afford for her to stay home. Wives just stayed home and the family lived on whatever their husbands earned. When Papa died Bubbie was left in bad financial shape. There was very little insurance money, just enough to pay for his burial, and Bubbie wasn't eligible for Social Security yet. She was still in her fifties, still full of energy and good-looking, and determined not to be alone for the rest of her life.

I knew she kept company. That's a funny concept: Bubbie dating. I have vague memories of the men who came calling on her. And she was engaged to a nice man named Mr. Feldman. He brought us toys and took all of us for rides in his brand-new Pontiac. He died just two weeks before the wedding. Then she met Mr. Rosenstein.

Before he came around I had never ever heard about how joint accounts work, *or* the value of prenuptial agreements. He was the man that she married and divorced. I had never heard of divorce before he came around, either.

They said that he was a wealthy man. Well, we are usually comparing one thing in life with another, so my family was probably comparing his station in life to ours. He lived in Flatbush, an upper-middle-class neighborhood; we were still living in Brownsville, a ghetto neighborhood. Where he lived there were tree-lined streets and private houses, and the shops were the best in Brooklyn. During their courtship Mr. Rosenstein took my grandmother shopping in his neighborhood, to the haberdasher's to have hats made just for her. This was impressive! It certainly imparted the information to everyone that this was a man of means. Who else would have hats made at the haberdasher's for his lady?

I think my grandmother liked him. It's hard to say for sure if she loved him. She hadn't loved Papa either when she married him. I do know that she thought if she married Mr. Rosenstein she could be financially comfortable into her last years of life. That was important.

Bubbie and Mr. Rosenstein were married and moved to Flatbush. They had a small wedding. My parents and my aunt and uncle chipped in to buy them china and silverplate (service for eight). Most of the furnishings that they had in the apartment were his. He had kept all the furnishings that he and his first wife had owned. She died years earlier. Nothing was replaced.

They went to Florida by train on their honeymoon. Bubbie was in her glory telling all her friends about their plans. Nobody in her crowd ever left New York State. They considered a trip to the Catskills an event. This was big-time. What a catch she had made.

When they came back from Florida, they busied themselves setting up house and establishing their day-to-day routine. They opened a joint account at the local bank. They deposited their money, as they had agreed, and received one passbook that represented all of her savings and part of his. It had both their names on it: *Mr. and/or Mrs. Rosenstein.* He was the businessperson in the family, so he took charge of the passbook. "Not to worry," he said; he would make sure that the interest was posted properly and that all the bills were paid. What a relief for Bubbie; she was proud and relieved. Life was going to be good. Of course, she missed my grandfather, but nothing could bring him back and now she and Mr. Rosenstein would share a decent life together.

Then it started. He was no longer courting Bubbie—she was his wife. He would take her to the refrigerator and show her the food that was there and explain how much she could have each day. He would cut an apple in half and let her know that the other half was for tomorrow. He told her how many phone calls she could make to her family and friends, and when he left her in the house, the story goes, he would put Scotch tape on the phone to see if she had used it while he was out. Not quite the fellow she'd thought she was marrying.

In the early days she told no one: she was ashamed. Finally she gathered her courage and went to her children with her story. It took everybody's breath away. She had no access to her money, no home but his. My mother and father had moved to Flatbush only a few months before, just a few streets away from Bubbie. "Come home," they said immediately. "Come to live with us."

And that is how when I was 10 my grandmother moved in with me to share my bedroom. She left Mr. Rosenstein. It took extraordinary courage. What would people think? She had her dignity and the small amount of money that she had brought to the marriage. Or did she? Maybe you guessed it. No, she did not! Mr. Rosenstein had taken all the money out of their joint savings account. The passbook that they had been given by the bank so many months before no longer existed. Everything had been placed in a new savings account in his name only.

Bubbie found this out when she went to the bank to retrieve her half of the money. She was advised by the officer at the bank, "I'm sorry, but if an account has both names on it, either person may remove the funds without the other's permission. As you knew, *the account had read EITHER/OR.* Either you or Mr. Rosenstein had complete access to *all* the money at any time." At first Bubbie was sure there had been a mistake, and in fact there had been: she had given her money up without understanding the implications of what she had done. Her husband hadn't done anything illegal. The bank hadn't done anything wrong. She was plain out of luck. She did get all the china from him, and half of the silverplate, but never the money.

No legal agreement had been drawn up before the marriage. There was an understanding: She would put all her money with his and they would live as a couple. He wouldn't put all his money with hers, though; he would only match what she put in—the rest he would keep separate. He would pay for the majority of what was required for their daily life; he was the person who would hold the money. Bubbie would always be taken care of. If Mr. Rosenstein died before her, his assets that he had kept "separate" would go to his grown children from his first marriage. That was only fair, Bubbie and he agreed. She got along well with his children. They were very happy that their father had someone to share his life with; they had no problem with their father's arrangements. The money that they had each put together in the joint account would be hers after the costs of his burial. That was the understanding. That wasn't what happened. They were divorced. She never remarried.

I don't think that Bubbie would have asked for a prenuptial agreement even if she had known about such a thing. She thought she was gaining much more than she could possibly lose. I also think, knowing my Bubbie, that it was too cold, too harsh an idea to discuss amidst notions of romance and marriage. A **prenuptial agreement** defines the financial parameters of a marriage. It often takes into account the possibility of illness, death, or divorce. It is prepared by a lawyer and signed by both parties. It is a contract written before anything goes wrong. It is a business agreement. Bubbie never thought of herself as a businesswoman.

Even some of us who do consider ourselves businesspeople shudder at the thought of turning romance and love into a business contract. My friend Eddie recently remarried. He's a lawyer who had been divorced for a long time, something like ten years. From time to time he'd talk about what he would do if he remarried, how he'd protect himself financially next time. Last time, he had no thought that a marriage of his would ever end. Next time he would know better. Last time, he was left with a lot of debt, and a lot less than what he considered to be a fair share of the assets that he and his wife owned. There was no way he was ever going to put himself in the same position again.

Not long ago we found ourselves talking about his new marriage over a cup of coffee. He looked at me sheepishly and said, "I just couldn't do it. I just couldn't approach the conversation with Janis about creating a prenuptial agreement. I didn't want her to think that I don't trust her; it just didn't feel like a nice thing to do.

"I decided to handle it another way. I decided that everything I had in my name alone before the marriage would stay in my name. Things that I buy or accumulate while we're married, I'll put in our joint name. We just bought a home and we put that in both names. Janis is also keeping separate the investments that she had before. It's really not as good as having a prenuptial agreement, and every state has its own divorce laws. Here in New York, as long as I don't mix the assets that I had prior to the marriage with what we accumulate now, they are considered to be separate from the assets of the marriage. If I mix it all together then it all may become part of the marriage. It would require some serious record keeping to prevent that result. That is, with the exception of a pension. If I have a pension and I am married ten years before we divorce, then she will be entitled to half of *all* of it. It's the best I felt I could do. At least in the state that we live in it works. In states where there are community property rules for divorce, the results may be different.

"As far as my death is concerned, well, that will be taken care of in my will. I have no children from my previous marriage, so that's not a problem. I will presume as of now that if I died I'd leave everything to Janis anyway. Well, close to everything—I'd want to leave something to my mom if she was still alive, and to my nieces and nephews. I haven't really discussed my will with Janis. She doesn't like to talk about my dying and I know she'll probably get upset if I tell her that I'm not leaving everything to her. Anyway, once we have kids things will change again, and there's no real reason to spoil how well things are going.

"I know that I said that I would handle things differently this time, but I'm betting that we're never going to get divorced, that's all."

We looked at each other and started to laugh. We were laughing at how sophisticated he had supposedly become, while still behaving in his old way. The media certainly has certainly made us aware of the kind of potential havoc a prenuptial agreement can bring. After all, didn't Jane Fonda and Ted Turner have to put their trip to the altar on hold so that they could deal with the business of marriage? Here Eddie was Mr. Legal and Mr. Fiscally Responsible, and he had made the decision not to have a prenuptial agreement. Yes, it is true that Donald and Ivana Trump had a prenuptial agreement and in the end she was reported to be very unhappy with what she considered an unreasonable and unfair agreement. But it was a place they could start negotiating from. I hope that the decision Eddie made will work for him and Janis. If he thinks that by not asking for an agreement he is showing that he loves his bride more than the men or women who do request a trip to the lawyer, I think not. If there are issues that need to be handled, then handle them or be prepared for potential problems in the future. Don't think that they will go away. Besides, shouldn't you be having conversations about money in general? There is more than a prenuptial agreement to be discussed. This is the person that you are committed to being with forever, the person you love and who loves you, and yet you are afraid to talk about something as important as money? What's the deal?

In days gone by, couples entered their first, and for many their only, marriage with nothing but commitment and devotion. Divorce was not common. Economics kept families together. Most young people built their finances together. Today there are many second and third marriages, second and third families. Life has become much more complex. Hallmark Cards has created a new line to address the new family members that we have accumulated in our extended families. Yet I guess that even with all this information, even with all the statistics thrown at us, we in the middle class are still like my friend Eddie. We consider a request for a prenuptial agreement a slap in the face. We like to think we are romantics. We don't want to talk about failing. We haven't been trained to handle these issues of money and love openly. Among those considered rich or who plan on being rich, it has nothing to do with romance. It is in the counting room, not the bedroom, that this matter comes into play.

Looking Good

"Looking good" can be a dangerous game to play!

In addition to everything else, money is a metaphor and an emotional emblem. That's why from time to time it makes us crazy. It's charged with all kinds of feelings. We use it as a measuring stick, a tool to determine if we are successful or not, if we are powerful or not, if we are like our parents or not. We use it to judge ourselves. We use it to judge others. We have feelings about money, and sometimes those don't feel so good!

Sometimes we are afraid of failing or looking bad. Oh, that "looking good" thing gets us in a big way. You know what I mean. We don't want anybody to think that we're not smart or together. We pay a big price for that. We should all have the privilege of getting help when we want it. But some of us don't like to speak up or reach out. We don't want anyone to figure out that we don't know everything or that we have made money mistakes. But nobody knows everything. We know that's a truth. We just don't want *them* to know! And they are running around not wanting *us* or anybody else to know.

"Looking good" can really do you in. Often in workshops women tell me what it is that others don't know about them and money: "I really don't have as much as people think," or "I've made a lot of money mistakes." The truth is that most people don't care, unless your money has a direct relationship to them. They have their own stories. They are probably too busy being concerned about looking good to you and everyone else in their lives. They deal with their own money concerns daily and have enough to worry about apart from you. You don't have to hold so tightly to those deep, dark secrets about yourself and money.

That doesn't mean you need to tell everybody your financial history. But try to realize that when and if you do tell someone, it will probably not affect how they view you as much as you imagine. They may even feel relief at having someone open up, giving them permission to do the same. There are people who care and will help and support you if you take the chance and reach out. You may find an opening to ask for guidance with friends and family; they may have been through a similar experience. They may have some good advice to share. Ask them for a referral to a financial adviser. Even if you don't want to tell them everything that is going on in your life financially, you can ask them to steer you to someone you can trust. Be willing to give up the "I'm in great shape, I look good" routine. Mostly, what I've found is that once your lack of financial ability has been bared in the light of day it is a lot easier to handle the problems and move on. But if we are more committed to "looking good" than to really dealing with our money issues, openly, we tend to make things worse. Know anybody like this? I do.

I have a very good friend who lives in Los Angeles. (Anyone reading this who lives in Los Angeles, please forgive me if you disagree, but that is one "looking good," make-believe city.)

Phyllis used to be a jingle singer. Hers was the voice we heard on many radio and TV commercials. Alas, over the last few years her singing style has become less fashionable. You know how it is. There's always a new hot sound. After having a great run singing her heart out for toothpaste and cereal commercials, she is now called to work much less than in the early years.

Phyllis is single, just past 40, and is dependent on her income not only to maintain herself but to help support her dad in a nursing home. He was a steelworker in a mill in Pennsylvania when she was growing up. When the mills shut down he took odd jobs doing home-repair contracting. Her mom had worked as a waitress. Neither of her parents had any retirement benefits from their employers. Her mother died about five years ago and shortly after Phyllis helped move her father to Los Angeles. He has Alzheimer's disease.

For the last two years Phyllis has taken money from her pension plan to help pay bills. When she started earning money she opened a pension plan and has contributed to it religiously every year. She was very proud and felt smart because she was planning ahead. That pension money meant hope for the future.

Now, each time she borrows money from her pension, she tells me that it's just this one time. I think she really wants to believe that that's true. But that isn't the way it's been. Each withdrawal makes her feel better for the moment—but only for a moment. After all, she has to pay taxes on the money that she takes out. The government has set very serious rules to discourage early withdrawal. If you withdraw from a pension or retirement plan before age 59½, you have to pay the government not only taxes but also a 10 percent penalty. If she keeps this up, Phyllis will be without any savings in three or four years.

She lives in a rented house that she used to share with her boyfriend. Now that they are no longer together, she carries all the costs of the house—the rent, utilities, telephone, and homeowner's insurance—by herself. Rental of a house has no tax benefit. If you own a home, you can deduct the mortgage interest each year. If you rent, there is no interest to deduct. There's always a silver lining, though: she's happy she doesn't have to worry about property values decreasing because of mud slides and fires. She doesn't have to worry about resale of the house.

She is also maxed out on her credit cards. She is starting to drown in a sea of debt.

Phyllis has a lot of pride. She doesn't want "them" to know that things are not as good as they used to be. She could move to a smaller place, but then people might think that she wasn't doing well. She has always been very generous with her friends on birthdays and holidays and there seems to her to be no way that she could cut back on that gift giving. After all, people are used to it. Her accountant knows, I know, and some really close friends know, but she could never tell "them." She just bought a crystal vase for a friend getting married. How could she not? What would they think? Well, I think: What a mess!

The other day I decided to play the "What if" game with Phyllis on the phone. "What if they didn't matter that much? What would you do?"

"I'd get a part-time job teaching English as a second language," she told me, "or use my computer skills to work part-time in an office. But if I was seen in this town doing anything but singing, people would know and my career could be over. If that wasn't the fact I would be able to do a lot of things. I'd move to a much smaller place. I could live with some friends for a while to cut my costs, or I could even take in a roommate . . . if I didn't care how it looked. I would stop buying new clothes to keep up my image. But in my world you need to keep things looking a certain way. If it didn't matter, maybe I would take more money out of my pension and go back to school. I always wanted to be a teacher; I just need a few more credits to graduate. I love kids. I could go to work with some friends to raise some extra money for now. But then I wouldn't be available if I got a call to work. That would finish my career completely. I just can't take the chance. I know I'm hardly working now, but I can't throw in the towel. Not only that—I know that I just need to wait a bit and things will turn around; I've been making all the right moves. Other friends have asked me to start a small business with them but I just don't want to, not yet. I know I'm right."

Some dilemma! After all, what would "the neighbors"—her professional colleagues—think? What does it really matter? Lots of people live in this world of "looking good," and are really hooked. We've all heard stories about famous entertainers or athletes who die penniless. But the stories about our not-so-famous family and friends go untold. Most people don't get to the stage of being totally without money, but a lot do wait until they have gotten into debt, declared bankruptcy, and experienced personal pain. And for what? In the end, there is a high price to be paid for "looking good."

So what's a person to do? Really think this through. What would life be like if you were able to change and stop worrying about how things look? Remember, you are stuck in behaving in a way that is comfortable. Yes, it's true that you would like to have things different, but are you prepared to be different? Are you hiding out and being stubborn about how things look? If you are, it could kill you!

There's a story I know about a preacher who was a very proud and religious man. His whole congregation looked up to him. One day it rained very hard and the town started to flood. The congregation began to make plans to evacuate. The preacher stayed at the church and told everybody to go ahead, that God would save him. The waters grew around him and he climbed to the roof. One couple from the congregation rowed past the preacher in a boat and called out to him, "Please come with us." "No," he said. "God will save me." He didn't want his people to think that he needed to get away in a boat. After all, he was the preacher. As the waters swelled higher, the preacher climbed to the steeple. A helicopter flew by. "Would you like some help, Pastor? Just hang on to the rope." "No," said the preacher again, "God will save me." And the preacher drowned.

When he got to heaven he was very upset. How could this have happened to him? What would the parishioners think of the fact that God had not saved him? Hadn't he done all the right things? This was not the way it was supposed to be. He wanted his parishioners to see him in a special light.

When God came to meet him he was so upset that he spoke to the Almighty. "Why didn't you save me? I did all the right things. I did everything that you could have possibly have wanted all the years that I served you. I told all my parishioners that you would save me and you failed me. You failed me in front of my parish. I ended up looking foolish."

"I tried," said God. "I sent a boat and a helicopter but you just wouldn't get on. You had to have things look a certain way."

Think about it: "Looking good" can cost you your life!

Please Read the Label

Are you one of those serious consumers? Do you know the terms of your adjustable rate mortgage, your credit cards, perhaps even your car lease? Do you save the instruction book for your telephone answering machine and calculator, and if you do, do you know where they are? Do you hold on to every receipt, documentation of transaction, and prospectus? Do you in fact know what those papers say? Do you remember what you wrote in your will, or for that matter where your will is, and do you understand it? Do you read and file important communication?

Do you read the labels?

Are you one of those people who think they know how to do things and take pride in not registering equipment with the manufacturer, only to have the computer go on the fritz and be helplessly embarrassed when speaking to a representative of the company? Do you get a simplified user's manual for your computer, only to let it gather dust on your bookshelf next to a host of other "how to" books that you have acquired in the past? Can you find the instruction manual for the things you have thrown out, but not for the equipment that you are having difficulty with?

Maybe you do save the booklets that you get with new purchases, but do you read them? If not, there is nothing to be embarrassed about. From what I can tell, you have plenty of company.

The other day Elaine, one of the women I work with, was telling me that she rarely balances her checkbook. She gets to it every six months or so. She just keeps extra money in the account so that her checks don't bounce. Are you one of those people? When she did sit down recently and opened her statements, she noticed that she had been charged a monthly service charge of $25 for the last three months for having a balance that dipped below her bank's minimum. The bank had notified her by mail that their minimum for free checking had gone from $3,000 to $6,000; she just hadn't taken the time to read that letter. She had tossed it aside to be looked at later, and that "later" had waited until now. She had just incurred $75 in charges.

Boy, was Elaine annoyed with the bank and the bank teller she talks to when she goes into the branch. (Yes, she actually goes into the branch and speaks to the teller.) She had never linked her checking with her savings, and that could have helped her out too, but she wasn't going to do that now. No way! She was moving her account. She was moving to a bank that required smaller minimums and had lower fees. She was also good-naturedly laughing at herself over the fact that she balances her checkbook every six months whether she thinks she needs to or not. Now you might say that she has enough money so that she doesn't need to balance her book, but that isn't the point. The point is that Elaine is one of the people who lives her life without reading the labels. Not bank or brokerage statements, not letters from the IRS, not much of any communication about finances. You know what I mean, those of you who wing it, knowing that it might cost you from time to time, like it did Elaine.

You might also say that for important things you do seek assistance. Sure, you might not know the terms of your credit cards or your homeowner's insurance, but you do get help when you need it. There are lots of good people like you who rely on accountants, attorneys, bookkeepers, and financial advisers to research and check things out for them. They know that left to their own devices they might create unnecessary drama and dilemmas for themselves.

Yes, I know. You seek help for most important things. This is a good thing to do. There are consultants whose jobs were created just for people like you who do not want to be busy reading the labels (the small print, the instructions, the details). However, and let me say this clearly, whether you have someone else who reads and reports to you or you do it yourself, if you do not read *all* labels, or are unwilling to follow *all* the instructions, contracts, specifications, or similar documents or do not understand what you are reading, *things could blow up in your face.* If you feel confused about what you are reading or hearing . . . then you are confused. If things are not happening the way you had thought they should . . . seek help. Don't wait for the explosion.

When I was a kid we used to go to the Catskill Mountains in upstate New York every summer. My parents and my Aunt Fran and Uncle Mac rented bungalows. My Bubbie rented a room. She used my Aunt Fran's kitchen.

One weekend Bubbie decided that she was going to make a special treat for her grandchildren. She was going to make potato latkes. It wasn't a holiday or anything, she was just feeling good. Off she went into the small kitchen to create a feast. Not much later she walked out of the bungalow, and she didn't look happy. She was annoyed with my Aunt Frances: her potato latkes weren't cooking well at all and the oil had a funny smell. She invited my Uncle Mac into the bungalow for his opinion.

"A funny smell, you say?" Uncle Mac got up and went into the bungalow to see what was going on. The place stunk of chemicals. "Oh my God, Mama! What are you using to cook here? Turn off the fire. What's going on here?"

Indignantly, my grandmother turned off the flame. "If Frances had bought good cooking oil, this wouldn't have happened. My pancakes are ruined. She could have used Crisco or Wesson oil, but she wanted to save money I guess and she bought this junk called Lest."

"Lest?" questioned my Uncle Mac. "Do you mean Lestoil?"

"Yes," Bubbie said, "and that doesn't cook good at all."

"Mama, Lestoil is a cleaning product! It could have blown us all up to bits. Did you read the label?"

"It said oil. How was I supposed to know?" replied an embarrassed and angry Bubbie. "It looked like what I needed. I just assumed it was. It said Lest oil. It said oil, didn't it?"

We got lucky. We could have been blown into tiny pieces. Here Bubbie thought that she was using a generic brand of cooking oil, and instead she was cooking with highly combustible material. Not only do we have to read the labels of things we use, but we need to *understand* what we are reading.

Of course, what Bubbie did was extreme—or was it? Haven't you had experiences in your own life that were costly or time-consuming because you didn't check things out first? Do you understand each prospectus or legal document even after you've read it, if in fact you have?

Neil and Steph went to Martha's Vineyard on vacation and fell in love with the area. Over the short week that they played and wandered through the village they shared their dream of buying a summer home there one day. But they were both just starting out in their respective businesses and they didn't even own a city home yet. They were newly married, in their early thirties. They wanted to have a family in the not-too-distant future and had lots of plans for the years that they would share together. Steph had a business that sold recycled children's clothing and toys. She and a partner had opened a shop about one year before. So far it had been a success and they had made a decision to keep their profits in the business for growth and expansion. Neil was an electrician; he had started working on his own about two years before. They were moving along on the path that they had envisioned for themselves.

On the last day of their stay they saw a sign advertising a seminar on time-sharing on the island. They could have a guaranteed place to visit on their vacations every year. The weather wasn't very good—it looked like it was going to rain—and the topic was interesting. Since they were unfamiliar with the concept of time-sharing they decided to attend. At noon that day they visited the address posted on the notice and listened as a local realtor and a representative of the time-sharing group spoke.

They were told that for $10,000 they could purchase a two-week time-share in a two-bedroom villa that had been built and was developed by the realtor for individuals who wanted a guaranteed place to visit every year. The time-share would be leased by the buyers and would be theirs for a thirty-year period, after which time it would return to the developer. There would also be annual maintenance charges that they would be responsible for. Their two weeks would be fixed for the same time each year and could be changed only through a swapping program with other people. Any time not used could be banked and saved for future use if there were weeks available. The realtor would help new buyers with financing.

They were very excited. After all, one week at the Vineyard had cost them in excess of $1,000. No doubt costs would be going up in the future. They would have all their future vacations guaranteed and, with the exception of the maintenance charges, paid off within a few years. They decided to buy the time-share. What a stroke of luck to have found this on the very last day of their vacation!

Neil and Steph signed the necessary papers, selected the two weeks that would be theirs (the week of and immediately after Labor Day), and went home tanned, rested, and fulfilled.

Because neither of them had borrowed from banks before or developed any strong credit references, they were advised that the realtor could assist them in getting a credit line to pay for their purchase. They would have to pay a premium rate. At the time banks and lending institutions were charging around 10 percent for mortgages, but this was not a mortgage on a residential property and if they wanted to borrow money they would have to get their loan from a commercial lending company through the time-share organization at 19 percent. They would be borrowing $9,000. Translated to the bottom line, this meant that they would be paying a very high rate of interest—$1,720 a year. That had nothing to do with paying down a penny of the $9,000 principal. However, the principal would also have to be paid out over 30 years.

After all the calculations, they realized they would be paying $2,500 a year in credit payments. That came out to $208 in monthly payments. Then there was $75 a month in maintenance charges, making a grand total of $283 a month. If you multiply that by twelve you will note that the two-week vacation was now costing our friends $3,396 a year. That was a lot more than they had bargained for. This would certainly put a kink in their budget. Had they thought about the deal more carefully they might not have gone ahead with it.

In the first place, unlike the interest on a mortgage for a first or second home, for which they would have gotten a tax deduction, there was no write-off for this debt. OUCH! Second, with the time share they would always be taking the same vacation at the same place. It would have been different if they had money for other vacations as well, but this was all they planned to spend toward vacations and, truth be told, it was turning out to be a lot more than they had ever planned to use for vacation money. Now they were locked into the same two weeks unless other people were interested in swapping with them. What had appeared to be the solution to a vacation question for them could easily become the last thing they wanted to bother with.

Notice that being together had not stopped Neil and Steph from making a choice that should have been better thought through. Sometimes there is danger in numbers. Agreement with a bad decision validates that decision. God knows we love agreement!

Emotion had taken the driver's seat, steering them into a tight spot. Had they understood what they were reading, they might not have bought at all. From the story they tell and retell, they were given all the information that they needed to make an informed choice. They just didn't understand what they were reading or hearing, not in the way that it needed to be understood to get the point. The facts had been presented properly; there was no misrepresentation. They had heard them the way they wanted to hear them so that they could make the decision to buy their time share.

Don't judge Neil and Steph too harshly. If we all haven't personally done something like this, most of us at least know someone who has.

No matter who you are, no matter what your education or social status, if you aren't clear about what you are agreeing to, you can find yourself in serious difficulty. No one is immune. Don't think age will protect you, either. Remember Bubbie; she had read that the bottle said Lestoil.

One of my very favorite people, an older gentleman named Stuart, tells me a story about an investment he made years ago with some of his friends. He laughs as he tells this story. Nice to have a sense of humor . . . an invaluable asset!

Both Stuart and Howard were retired from their jobs. They had been widowers for about the same length of time, their children were grown, and they always hung out with each other. They had been great friends since childhood. They bought their homes in the same town, went to the same church, and hung out with the same crowd. They were a natural duo.

Anyone who knew these two guys would think that when it came to making investments they would probably be willing to do something like buying a horse together. Actually, they each bought one-tenth of two racehorses.

Stuart loved horses and he knew how valuable a good horse could be—not from firsthand experience, but he had heard. He had heard lots of stories about the owners of horses winning big purses. The life surrounding the world of horses seemed very exciting too.

Wouldn't it be wonderful to sit in a box and watch a horse you owned run a race and win? So when Howard suggested that they invest in the new foals of a horse from a breeder they met, Stuart agreed. In fact it wasn't quite as snap a decision as I have implied, but it didn't take that much more time either. There are some things that you just have to feel with your gut and go with, and according to both men this was one of them.

Stuart assumed that Howard had researched the investment thoroughly, and Howard assumed that the breeder had things in hand. Howard had met the horse breeder at his niece's place only the weekend before. Neither of these two fine men had a clue as to how much risk they were about to undertake. They hadn't given their financial advisers or attorneys any documents to read because they trusted the horse breeder and because they didn't want to miss out on this opportunity. I might add that they didn't want anyone to suggest that they rethink this course of action. Only twenty investors would be allowed to participate in the deal. Perhaps their advisers would not appreciate the beauty of this deal. So after a cursory overview Stuart and Howard signed the papers and were in the horse-racing game.

By now you know that I wouldn't be telling you this story unless I wanted to make a point. After the stories of Bubbie and Neil and Steph you may have guessed the point I'm driving at. But I'll say it anyway. The foals weren't of the caliber of their mother or their father. Nice horses, pretty horses—but nowhere near the strength and speed they needed to be trained for racing.

Although the foals no longer needed special trainers once the decision was made not to train them for racing, they still needed to be fed and housed. And guess who was partially responsible for their care. You got it: my friend Stuart and his best friend Howard. Nice that they can laugh. I guess that's what some of us do when there is nothing left to do. At first they were shocked that not only would they not be watching their horse win the Kentucky Derby, but until the horses were sold they would be responsible for the care of these new little guys. They had signed the agreement saying that they understood their financial obligations. I'm not sure that they really did read what they signed. If they did, they sure didn't plan on the horses' being anything but winners.

In the end Stuart says, it's an expensive story to tell. But they sold the horses, recouped part of their money, and are here to tell the tale. Stuart says it's Howard's fault, and Howard says that he had bet Stuart would be more responsible before jumping in up to his neck. Both of them love to talk about what could have been. Wouldn't it have been incredible to be an owner of a horse that won the Kentucky Derby? Both men agree they probably never would have made this investment if their wives were still alive. The women would have asked too many questions and read every little piece of paper!

You Gotta Be in It to Win It

Ever meet one of those people who talk all the time about what could have been? The ones who could have been the best athlete, the best writer, the best of everything and anything? Maybe they could have, but they never even got in the game. They live in a fantasy world of how it could have been, but never even get up to the plate. I don't like being around these people very much; they're boring and usually inauthentic. I prefer people who go for it.

It's much more exciting to be on the playing field than rooting on the sidelines. Regardless of how great your bleacher seats are, or how big a fan you are, the greatest rush and joy in winning is always the player's. The player puts himself at stake; the victory is his or hers.

Don't you enjoy being around people who can tell you about how they went for it? Can't you picture their faces as they replay their special moments? These memories are etched forever, bringing the energy of life to their stories. It doesn't matter whether it was a love, a job, or an athletic triumph. It is of no significance that the adventure did not change the shape of the nation. What matters is that going for the gold enabled the person to experience winning and losing—the depth of life itself.

Each time we personally experience taking risks and really going for it, we learn. Taking chances, being at risk, and being in the game move us from spectator rank to player. But what about the risk of not doing anything? What about the risk of not risking?

You mean there is risk in not risking? Uh-huh. So you must mean that we are always risking? Right again.

When we fill out the questionnaire about risk (see front of this section) in my workshops, the women who participate frequently respond the same way. Their answers sound like these:

> *The places I have taken risk in my life are . . . relationship,*
> *   and career.*
> *Usually when I take risks in my life the results are . . . good,*
> *   great, rewarding.*
> *I am more apt to take risks if . . . I am not afraid . . . I*
> *   understand what can happen.*
> *Taking risks with money means . . . being prepared to lose . . .*
> *   having no control . . . being afraid.*
> *Talking about taking risks makes me feel . . . excited, alive,*
> *   tentative, and nervous, nauseous.*
> *If I take risks then I . . . will grow, mature, be alive, win.*

We notice that when we talk about taking risks there is a special electric charge in the air. People sit up taller and there is a sense that exciting things are about to take place.

As we begin to look at our personal histories related to risk, we notice that we women are the specialists in relationship risk—not just intimate relationships, but family and friendship stuff. We have had much more experience with our lovers, family, and friends than with most other things. Probably, that's how we were programmed. As women we are supposed to be the leaders in taking those kinds of risks, and we do. We reach out to family even if we are unsure of the reception we may find. We initiate talks with our friends about expanding, improving, or ending our friendships. We give our hearts away over and over again.

We know that losing at relationships is always possible and can be painful. We have all experienced that seldom graceful art of surrendering when we realize that we are not going to be successful at sustaining a relationship that we have been struggling over. However, most of us still get up to bat yet another time and even go for the home run: the committed relationship, the wedding band, the new baby. We may take time out to heal our wounds, but sooner or later we are back out there at the plate.

In business and careers too we women have taken risks. We have applied for positions that we had once assumed were unavailable to us. We have been in charge of meetings, handled employers and employees, juggling family and work schedules. We have been at risk, and have won and lost, but still we stay in the game.

We were trained as relationship specialists, we have been training ourselves to be career specialists, but so far we have spent relatively little time training in the money game. As a result we understand a good deal about what happens when we win or lose in relationship and career, but as yet very little about risk and money. Still, the more understanding we gain of our fears about risk and money, the sooner we can deal with them and feel the excitement and enthusiasm, the possibilities that exist when we finally do get up to the financial bat for our home run.

Money represents survival. We buy our food and our shelter with money. We negotiate for services and pay for almost everything with money; few people work on a barter exchange basis in this country. And even though we don't always use those paper dollars anymore, each check, credit card, and ATM transaction represents money. If we understand this truth—that we are already deep in this money game we don't always understand—then it's easy to see the value of getting to be a decent player.

What is it that makes women so uncomfortable about risk? This issue comes up again and again, so let's really get down and talk about the feelings that women have about risk and money.

Do you ever experience the fear of not having enough or of losing everything? Or is it just that the subject of money makes you feel overwhelmed and you can't stand the feeling of being out of control? Each one of us has had at least one or more conversations with ourselves about risk and money. I see over and over again in my daily life as a financial adviser, and most definitely in my workshops, that there are lots of women who feel ignorant on the subject of money and who would rather not risk looking stupid or foolish. They own up to the fact that they sometimes just don't understand.

Lots of women don't like the power struggle attached to money negotiations. They may understand what's at stake but not want to risk looking tough or bitchy. In our unwillingness to risk being seen in what we may have been taught or persuaded is a negative light, we may risk not even getting up to the plate.

Regardless of the underlying reason—and sometimes it's more than one—we can get stopped in the dugout, never even taking the chance of lifting the bat or throwing the ball.

Sometimes we step up to the plate and take our swings, what I would consider a risk, and we strike out. We don't give ourselves enough credit then for the risk we've taken! It's as though if we don't get a win, then the entire experience is bad, forgettable. How different from when we are in our relationship mode, where we are more likely to use each experience as an opportunity to learn for the next time.

Often we do take risk and don't even realize that we have in fact dealt with risk and money. We buy a car and arrange credit. Or we buy a home. We don't think that that's such a big deal. After all, we got through it okay. We may have been slightly ill at ease, but not actually ill, and as a result we don't reflect that we did in fact go to bat and hit a single. In fact we seldom look back at that stuff unless something goes wrong . . . and sometimes it does. If in fact the real estate market should go to hell as it did in the late eighties, then we get an opportunity to judge what fools we were for taking that kind of risk. Otherwise we don't take credit for the things that proceed as business as usual.

I have two clients, Judy and Marvin, who graduated from business school in the early eighties, married, got jobs, and saved enough money to buy an apartment near their office at the height of the real estate market. They paid top dollar for their small one-bedroom co-op in Manhattan. Of course when they bought it there appeared to be no risk. In those days everybody knew that the value of real estate would always go up, there would always be a way to sell and get your money out. At a minimum, you would always get back at least what you paid. That's what everybody thought back in 1987.

In 1993, just six very different years later, they discovered that the apartment no longer suited them. They were earning more money and expecting a baby. They found out from various brokers that there was no market for a small one-bedroom apartment. The market was glutted with them. Not only that, but their co-op rules said that they could not sublet. They had mortgage payments that were much larger than the current market value of the apartment could recoup. They felt awful. Actually Marvin felt bad and Judy was mortified. A business school graduate, and she was really looking dumb now.

Marvin didn't feel stupid; he just felt that they had a bad business break. He had never experienced a real estate market like this in his adult lifetime, and he figured he had now learned plenty that he could use for future reference. Marvin felt that they should sell the apartment and get out. If they had to, they would take a loss and buy another place. They couldn't rent it because they were not permitted to sublet. The co-op had to stay owner occupied or empty. In any case, they needed the money so they could reinvest what was left in something new. Thank God they had enough money to move on. They would use the soft real estate market as an opportunity and make the best of not the best situation. They had gotten in at the wrong time, but things would work out.

Judy, on the other hand, was questioning her and Marvin's ability to make a good investment decision. She felt that they had taken a risk and struck out. Maybe they shouldn't try to get up to bat again. Maybe they just weren't meant to own a home. Maybe they should just rent. Maybe they shouldn't sell at a loss. She didn't want to live in a one-bedroom apartment with a baby, but maybe that was the price for making a bad choice. She even worried that her parents would be disappointed in their daughter, the business school graduate.

Now mind you, way back when they bought the place, they never thought that there was much risk in buying real estate. They had not focused on the fact that there is always **risk of loss of principal** if the value of the property goes down—and that can happen. They also had an adjustable mortgage that adjusted every year in relation to the rate of the five-year Treasury bond. They didn't think much about the fact that the rate might go up, but in fact it did for a while, causing them to have higher mortgage payments. Oh, **interest rate risk.** And then there was the possibility that Judy had never even thought about: that there might be no buyer at all. They had never thought of **liquidity risk.** No buyer means no sale, and that means not getting out of ownership of the apartment. She and Marvin had put themselves at risk without ever really thinking about it. The real estate market was strong and had been getting stronger every day. The truth is had things gone as they had expected, they might never have thought about the risks they had taken at all. They would have just sold this place and moved on to the next. Now Judy was scared to death about taking a similar risk.

Marvin said that in fact they hadn't focused on what could go wrong, but of course he had known all about these things. He had thought Judy knew that these kinds of things happen too, and that that should not stop them from buying another place. This was a lesson and they would use it to their advantage. As best I could see, Marvin was more adept at handling personal business risk. They had experienced the same result but had drawn different conclusions. Judy took her experience as a personal reflection of who she was as a person. She was wiping out all her positive and correct choices with this one strikeout.

Marvin and Judy finally agreed to sell the apartment if they could, taking the expected loss, and buy another place anyway. The real estate market was soft, so they hoped to get a house or larger apartment at a decent cost too. That was the other side of the coin: they could get a good deal on something else if they sold and bought at the same time. It took all of Judy's courage to go for it. Since then, it appears that their choice was a sensible one. The market for real estate is getting better, and the value of their new place is going up as they had hoped. Had they not decided to buy something else, they would have missed the opportunity to have a positive investment experience.

More than making money on this new property, Judy learned to look at risk and understand her relationship to it. It's proven very interesting! Whereas she was always able to understand the concept of risk in class, in an intellectual way, now she's integrating it into her own world. That is what makes it feel like a new concept.

When I was younger and had just started to work as a financial adviser, I had $500 to invest. I wanted my money to grow. I realized that although it wasn't a lot, it was all I had, and by making that investment I was putting everything I had at risk. I asked some of the other people in my office for their opinions about what to do with my money. Finally I made a decision to buy ten shares of a $50 stock. The name of the company was General Instrument. I'll never forget the name of that company, just like I'll never forget the name of my first lover. I knew that this was considered to be a high-risk stock. The company was involved in a new technology, but if they got the new business they were expecting, they would be worth much more. My main thought was: Am I prepared to lose my money? In any stock or investment you have to be prepared to lose. *If you are not pre-pared to lose any money, do not invest in stocks.* There are investments with no risk of principal. They may have other kinds of risk, like **not keeping up with inflation.** For example, if inflation is growing at 5 percent and the money is invested at 4 percent, even though you will not lose principal, your buying power will erode 1 percent each year. You may get to hold the same dollar in your hand as you did before, but it will buy you less. Sometimes this happens with bank accounts, money markets, bonds, and certificates of deposits, depending on what rate you receive.

I knew that I was prepared to lose some money if I was wrong about this stock. I also knew that I was prepared to put all my money into this one investment. And I did. It turned out that I made a 25 percent return on my money in one year: $125. Of course, the stock went up and down over the course of that year, and my stomach had more than one bumpy ride. I sold the stock and took a profit.

That was then. I was 31 years old. I had a different perception of what I was willing to risk and how. If I still wanted to buy an indi-vidual stock, I might do what I did all over again under the same cir-cumstances. It was a different time in my life. The investment was made with thought and I had chosen a quality company in the field I had selected. I had a small amount of money to invest and I was willing to take higher risks for higher reward. I was also aware of the potential losses I faced. Today, I wouldn't invest all my money in one place. In those days I figured that I had to start somewhere. I could have chosen a mutual fund, but I wanted to be an investor in an indi-vidual stock. I felt that the $500 I had would not change my current lifestyle or determine my future. I felt I had time on my side, so I decided to take an investment risk. Today, eighteen years later, 100 percent of my money is a lot more than I would want to put in one place. I'm older, I have more money invested, I have less tolerance for losses both financially and emotionally.

Sometimes people get a stock tip from a friend (or an acquain-tance or maybe somebody they met at a cocktail party) and with no other information they buy the recommended stock. This is a risky way to make an investment. It's different from taking an investment risk. It may or may not turn out okay. That's not the issue. If the stock doesn't go up, or worse, if it goes down, and they can't get any information from the person who gave them "the tip," they get frustrated and upset. They'll say they invested and had a bad experience in the stock market. Wrong: this was not an investment, it was a gamble based on hearsay.

Here in fact is a good tip about investing in the stock market: *Always assume that you are the very last one to be hearing a hot stock tip at a cocktail party or from the friend of a friend.* Then don't buy anything until you've done your research. You may risk not making money, but I can personally guarantee you won't lose any either.

If you do decide to take any kind of investment risk, understand what you are risking and how it will really affect you.

What's important is that you don't write off the game or the opportunity to become a pro. You can't get up at bat once and call it a game, and you can't take a shot at the World Series if you haven't won the pennant. In order to be in the game you have to risk striking out, looking bad, and maybe even feeling uncomfortable. But the glory of winning has its merits, and you've got to be a player to even have a chance at winning.

The Price of
Having to Be Right

Don't we all know people who make a mistake and then compound it by trying to fix it themselves? How about the ones who just can't admit that they made a mistake in the first place? I mean the people who just need to be right about certain things. No matter what, these diehards just won't give up. The price can be pretty high for wanting to be right about something, especially things you know next to nothing about. Alas, I'm speaking from personal experience.

I have red hair. It's not the color I was born with, but it is the color I've had for the last couple of years. I got it by accident, if you can believe such a thing; the accident happened because I was stubborn. Maybe it wasn't an accident after all.

Around my thirtieth birthday, I started noticing some gray hairs. No big deal, just something to notice. By 40 there were more than a few. I had always thought that gray hair was attractive and was sure I would never feel the urge to alter my hair color. But at the age of 42 or 43, I don't remember exactly when, I started having red highlights added to my hair to "give it some life." That process needed to be done every three months. But, at age 45, when I decided that my whole head needed coloring, I made the decision to do it myself. I didn't have the time to waste in a hair salon one day a month, and I didn't want to pay what I considered a lot of money for something I thought I could do as well myself. I went to a store on Eighth Avenue in Manhattan that sells beauty supplies and they helped me select hair dye that would provide we with a medium-brown hair color with a reddish tint. Just what I was looking for, a piece of cake. What did I need to waste time in a salon for?

Well, eventually there came a turning point in my career as a hair colorist. After visiting my children in Saskatchewan over the July Fourth holiday, I came home jet-lagged and cranky. It had rained almost the whole week there and I was not in a good mood! The next day was work and back to the old routine. It was one in the morning but I was still functioning on the Midwest clock and I wasn't very tired. I might as well color my hair and get that done, I thought; then I won't have to bother with it later in the week. Nothing like being efficient! Out came my little bag of tricks: my applicator and my developer and hair coloring. Forty minutes later I was tucked under the covers ready to dream sweet dreams.

The next morning when I went into the bathroom to get ready for work and brush my teeth, I noticed my hair. The roots were shades lighter than the rest of it. I realized what must have happened. The index card that I had written the preparation recipe on wasn't with me, so I decided to use my memory in preparing the mixture. I have a good memory and was almost sure what the combination was. Perhaps I should have waited until I found the card with the recipe. It appeared now that I might not have used the best judgment. Well, anyway, I'd fix it. After work I was going to get my hair trimmed, and right after that I'd come home and redo it all. Which I did.

When I looked in the mirror, I hated the new color. It was much too dark. Still not admitting defeat, I told myself I'd fix it again after work. This time I added more peroxide to the mix. Not much change. For the next three nights I came home with no more information about what I was doing than I had before and embarked on my color-of-the-night project. I didn't have a clue about what I was doing, what I was doing had not been working, and yet I expected different results. I had done no research and asked no one for assistance. What did I think would be the outcome? What's so fascinating about this experience is that during the entire process I had the capacity to sit back and observe myself and notice that in fact my behavior was incredibly stubborn and stupid. I could in fact lose all my hair, and yet I was unwilling to change my MO. I don't prescribe medication for myself, I use doctors. I hire attorneys and accountants, plumbers and paperhangers, because I think that they know their trade just like I know mine. But here I was, playing with chemicals, changing colors, and acting as if I knew what I was doing. If you watch television they tell you it's very easy, and it sure looks easy—so how come it wasn't so easy?

The next day, which was a Saturday, I visited the local drugstore and enlisted the assistance of the salesclerk behind the counter. "What can I do to lighten hair?" "Try Copper Penny," she said. So I did. That was the last straw. My scalp had had enough and so had I. In fact, I had a head of hair that was exactly the color of an old, brassy copper penny.

It was time to surrender. After making calls to some friends in the know, I made an appointment with a chic hair salon. The best they could do to start with was lighten my hair to a color that looked somewhat like Lucille Ball had picked it. But over the next few weeks and after many visits to the salon my hair became a fashionable reddish blond. What an ordeal, and I had brought it all on myself.

We call people professionals because they have been trained. I am not a professional hair colorist and when I noticed that I was on the road to no return I should have stopped and changed my game plan.

We don't know everything and we can't know everything. Sometimes we forget that. Sometimes we forget it at the most inopportune times. While all this was going on I kept thinking, I'm just like the people who keep buying stocks they heard about at the cocktail party and never make money investing in them. They haven't done any research, they haven't asked anyone for advice about the stock, they haven't even heard of the company before, and most often the person giving them the tip (much like the nice lady who told me to try Copper Penny) has no clue what they are doing either. Or better yet, I'm like the person who buys a stock and holds on to it while the price is plummeting. With no evidence or reason, they buy more on the way down, they do no research and wait while the value drops all the way down, and they keep telling themselves that things will eventually turn around. There are statistics showing that a stock changes hands much more often on the way up than on the way down. The individual holding the stock on the way down just lives with hope that things are going to be better. Successful professionals advise clients to buy low, sell high, and hold on if the stock is good. That is very different from buy and hold no matter what. Some investors just hold on wanting to be right. Getting professional advice is very important if you don't know what you are doing. Knowing when to take a profit and a loss is important. Knowing how to color your hair is important. The stakes are too high to fool around. The price for wanting to be right all the time can be too high.

One day my neighbor's dad stopped by to talk. He was visiting from Florida, where he and his wife retired to about ten years ago. Neither of them has a pension; they live on a fixed income—their Social Security check and the interest from their investments. Dale had been a salesman in the carpet business and Hanna had run a small day care center for children. They buy supplemental health coverage and belong to an HMO. Both of them are in fairly good health and have part-time jobs at the local department store, she in ladies clothing and he in small appliances. Both are in their early seventies and are delighted to live in the warm climate. Once or twice a year they see their children, who still live up north, one in New York and the other in Boston. They buy senior citizen discount coupons with the airlines and use them to fly to visit friends and family.

"I want you to know how happy I am with our investment adviser," Dale was telling me. "He's just the best. Treats us like family. Calls us Hanna and Dale. He makes a point of calling at least two or three times a week."

"That's really nice," I said, wondering where the conversation was leading.

"Anyway, he did just fine by us. Last year when an opportunity came up for us to buy a piece of property near our kids we called him and he lent us the money. Well, not exactly him. We borrowed it from his firm. Put up the stock and bonds we own as collateral and borrowed against our own investments. It will work out just fine. We expect to fix up the house and resell it. Make a quick profit, and turn things around. My son-in-law says it's a sure thing.

"Now our guy, our broker, was really concerned. He made sure that we understood that this is called **borrowing on margin.** When you borrow on margin you finance part of your stock purchase with money from the brokerage house that you are doing business with. We collateralized our loan with our stock and then borrowed half of the value. You pay interest at market rates to the bank or brokerage house that lends you the money. You don't have a fixed time frame in which to pay the money back. If the value of the stock should go down you may have a **margin call.** That means that you have to come up with money to bring the value in the account to the minimum requirement. He sent us a book to read and some papers to sign. We didn't read the book or papers; we trust him. What's the point of having an adviser if you can't trust them? Actually, interest rates have gone up since we borrowed the money. I thought that the rate was locked in at the time we took the money. It probably explained it in the book. Oh well, it's costing a little more than we planned, but it will be worth the profit on the house when we sell it."

"When are you planning on selling the house?" I asked. I had just put down coffee and some muffins for us to have. I could see this was going to be a lengthy visit, and I was hungry.

"Well, it's taking longer than we had thought. You see, my son-in-law and his friend both work in the construction industry. Well, business started to get a little busier for them and they didn't want to give up the work, so they work on our place on the weekends and do their regular jobs during the week. It looks like they might not be finished for another couple of months. That's longer than we would have liked, but I trust my son-in-law will get it done as soon as humanly possible. Then again, things are costing a bit more than they had anticipated. They call it 'cost overrun.' I can't imagine that it will be that much more, and I don't like them to think that I'm meddling in their business, so I try not to ask too many questions. His business partner is a genius. He buys and sells commodities. Knows all about gold and silver and things like that. Last month he told us to buy gold. I called my adviser and he told me it was very risky. He said that I could lose my entire investment trading commodities. They are very risky. He advised against it for people in our situation. I went ahead anyway. We had to sign some more papers, which we did. We made some good money taking my son-in-law's partner's advice. We made 40 percent on our investment in two days. Not bad, huh?"

I offered him a muffin. "Would you like butter or jelly?"

He was still wrapped up in his story. "Have you ever done that for people? Made that kind of a return that quickly? We were pretty smart. My guy wasn't happy with us at all, being that we live on a fixed income and all, but he couldn't argue with the results, now could he?"

"Well, that's very risky," I replied gingerly. "Can you afford to lose? I'm not in a position to give you advice based on knowing almost nothing about you, but trading commodities is a volatile and high-risk situation. Your adviser sounds like he was very right in warning you."

"Oh yes, he belongs to our church group and knows that we are very conservative people. I can't stand risk at all, but this idea was foolproof—my son-in-law's friend does it all the time—and we made enough money to pay the margin charges for months. Now I don't have to worry about paying those extra interest costs.

"Listen, I can't really stay long; just wanted to drop by and say hello and talk my investment strategy over with you. Hate to run, but we're going to visit our kids in Boston. If you like I could let you know the next time we do some trading."

"It's really nice visiting with you, and no thanks about those commodities—they're too risky for me." We said good-bye.

After he left I felt sad. From what he had told me he and Hanna were putting themselves and their savings in real jeopardy. I thought I should say something to their daughter.

She was well aware of the situation. "There's nothing you can tell them. They don't want to hear it. Their adviser has tried and so have I. We have to just let them do their thing."

A year later, my doorbell rang and it was my neighbor's dad. Dale and Hanna were up north again visiting, and apparently I was part of the rounds they were making. I thought I should just get the coffee on and listen.

"Well I guess you know that we still haven't sold that damn house up in Boston," Dale began. "The market there is very soft. 'Soft' means that you can hardly give away the damn thing. That's what my son-in-law says. Rentals are good but sales aren't, so we need to do something fast. If we rent, then I'm afraid if a buyer comes along we won't be able to vacate the house, and then I don't want the renter ruining the new work that just got done. There's not a night that goes by that I don't lose sleep over these things."

I offered them coffee.

"And the problem is that we still are paying that charge on the money we borrowed. It's a crime. Here we are making 5 or 6 percent on our investment and paying over 9 percent lately for our money. In the meantime, because interest rates went up, the value of our bonds went down. That's what happens when rates go up. Why should someone want to pay me a dollar for a bond that is paying 7 percent when they can buy bonds that are paying 8½ percent for the same money? If we sell our bonds to cover the loan, we lose money on that. We need to hold our bonds to maturity to be sure that we get our money back, or hope that rates go down again so we can sell them. Even though margin charges are deductible against interest income, it's not much help to us—we are in a real low tax bracket. Our financial adviser has been really concerned, and he should be. He should have explained all this to us last year before this whole mess started."

I didn't miss a beat. "I'm so sorry to hear you're having a problem. I thought that your adviser did discuss these risks with you."

"Problem? Are you kidding? We're drowning. The last two commodities trades we did we lost a pile of money. We lost more in those two transactions than we made together the whole year before. My son-in-law's partner is some gambler. My son-in-law should have told us what a nut this guy is. Sure, our broker told us, but I never expected things to be such a mess."

"I see."

"Anyway, I spent my whole life not trusting anybody and now I know why. Nobody cares about my things like I do. If we get out of this, I will never listen to anyone else."

"I really hope that things work out. Would you like more coffee?"

"No thanks, and I've gotta go now. Thanks for your advice; I love talking to you."

I hadn't given him any advice, but he wasn't kidding.

Do you really think that if we had the right advice in every situation, it could keep us from doing some of the things we do?

Facts We Learned:

RISK

There is more than one kind of risk in investing:
1. Principal
2. Liquidity
3. Inflation
4. Interest rate
5. Opportunity

Retirement plan distributions taken before age 59½ are subject to penalty as well as income tax.

Each state has its own laws governing distribution of assets that affect divorce negotiations.

Investment in commodities trading can bring loss up to 100 percent or even greater than the original investment.

Borrowing on margin means that you are collateralizing your securities at a brokerage house or a bank and using the funds to either buy additional securities or remove the cash from the account.

Remember: Don't put all your eggs in one basket. Practice diversification and asset allocation.

Lessons We Learned:

RISK

We are always at risk.

There are many components of risk:
>   the risk of not looking capable
>   the risk of not trying
>   the risk of not asking
>   the risk of not understanding

Our perception of risk changes as we gain knowledge about ourselves and what we are dealing with.

VI.

CHOICES

CHOICES

1. I feel _____ about the money choices I have made in the past.

2. Having to make choices about financial matters makes me feel _____.

3. The way that I choose to do things is based on _____.

4. When I'm given choices I prefer to _____.

5. I have little choice when it comes to _____.

6. I have plenty of choice when it comes to _____.

7. Choice has played a _____ part in my life.

Choices

You pick the game and how you will play,
You pick the rules and what you will say,
If you don't like your choice, then pick once more—
That's what choices are really made for!

You can say yes, or say no, or maybe just wait:
You are the one who determines your fate.
So choose for yourself, be safe and secure . . .
You hold the keys to open each door!

Ask the Stupid Questions

Don't you just love children? They tell it like it is. At the end of my last trip to Canada visiting my kids I was talking to my sweet grandson Tyler.

"I'm going to miss you so." Every day this wonderful little boy came down to my room and woke me up. "How am I going to get up on time when I go home?" I said.

"Don't you have a husband?"

I smiled and shook my head. "No."

"Then I think that you should get a clock, Grandma York."

A simple solution, straight to the point. No big deal. And he didn't get mad at me for asking a *stupid question.* What a kid. Had I asked another adult that question, I would have probably gotten a very strange look in response. After all, I would have been expected to know better. Which of course I did, but that didn't bother Tyler. Anyway, let's say I didn't have the answer. I might have gotten a complicated response from another grown-up: "Why would you want me to make your decisions for you?" Or "How have you been managing in the past?" Kids don't get that deep. They just answer the question. How nice!

Most little kids haven't had time yet to learn how to make simple problems into complicated ones. And they don't mind questions— that is, as long as you don't torture them. In fact, they get the point— they love to ask questions themselves.

Children operate with an understanding of basic rules that we sometimes forget or don't feel entitled to.

If you have a question to ask and feel stupid about asking it . . . it's the right question to ask! Kids ask all kinds of questions and they're seldom ashamed. They don't think they are asking stupid questions. That's how they learn. It's only after we have our hands on them long enough that they start to label some questions stupid. How can you be stupid if in fact you were never taught the information in the first place. *In fact, it's very smart to ask all the questions, especially the stupid questions, in the beginning.* All the good businesspeople I know ask millions of questions. They love asking questions; that's how they learn and continue to grow.

Many successful people put together teams to support them in accomplishing their goals. They depend on their associates to counsel and explain things to them. Think of the wise kings and queens who have sat on their thrones seeking counsel and asking their advisers. We can't know everything. Nor do we have to be specialists. That's what other people are for.

If trying something new and different scares you, say so. Don't be embarrassed . . . you can be grown up and still get scared. Sometimes being scared comes from not knowing or understanding clearly. Sometimes it comes from understanding very well that what is being posed to you is just *not* what you want to do. If you don't want to do something, then don't. Trust your instincts!

If you start doing something one way and it's not working for you . . . *try another way.* There are loads of ways to get to a destination. Be creative and look at all your choices. *Be willing to change.*

If you don't like the people you are playing with, you can pick new partners. Kids know that if they don't like the way they are being treated they can pick new playmates. We grown-ups think that just because we or other members of our family have had a relationship for years with an adviser, an accountant, or a lawyer, we have to stick with them. Not so—you get to choose. You are entitled to have whoever you want take care of you.

Marianne was really upset. She had just come back from meeting with her accountant and her parents. She was thirtysomething and still using her parents' tax adviser. Of course, she was successful at her job and could afford to go to her own person—it had nothing to do with that—but her parents got upset every time she brought up the idea of her not using Richard.

What upset her was that when she was at the meeting she felt about 8 or 9 years old. Maybe 10. They spoke around her and about her but not to her. When she did ask a question about her tax return, Richard would tell her not to worry and give her a knowing wink. He thought she was someone to be ignored. Wink at this, Richard, she thought, but she didn't say a word. It wasn't worth it!

Recently she had been talking with friends about tax planning. She knew that there was no question that she had to pay taxes. The question was how she could reduce them.

She decided to look around for another accountant on her own. Richard probably wouldn't have treated her like a child if he hadn't known her since she was a baby. But she was no baby anymore. She owned her own small advertising consulting firm. She deserved to be treated like an adult. In the meantime she would keep her decision from her parents.

A good friend referred Marianne to an accountant who specialized in working with small-business owners. "I have some stupid questions," she started out.

"Ask away," Ira, the accountant, replied.

"Is it better to make investments in things that are tax free or tax deferred?" This whole area was confusing to her.

"They are most often used for different purposes. **Tax free** means that whatever interest you earn is never taxed, not ever," Ira explained. You get the interest as it is paid. On the other hand, **tax deferred** means just that: deferred into the future. You will owe the money someday.

"Usually income from municipal bonds is tax free. If the bond is issued by your state, then you don't have to pay any federal or state taxes; if it is not from your state, then you just get a federal exemption.

"Now as far as tax deferred is concerned, the reason that the taxes are deferred into the future is that you probably do not have the use of the money now. Those things usually pertain to retirement accounts or annuities (that's an insurance product).

"In both cases," he continued, "keeping as much money in your pocket as possible is a valuable idea, and because you are in a high tax bracket you might want to use both ways. Do you have a retirement plan?"

"I do. I've had it for the last four years, ever since I started my own business. I make contributions for both me and my assistant. I don't know the name of it, though. I'm pretty embarrassed to tell you."

"No need to be embarrassed. Let me see the papers you brought with you about your existing plan and I'll explain them. I promise you, I know little about advertising."

She was starting to get a little more comfortable. Not quite enough, though.

Ira glanced through her papers. "You have what is called a profit-sharing plan. I see that you have been putting money away for the past four years."

Marianne took the paper back timidly. She had lots more questions but her head was spinning. "I think I better get some education on the subject here. I feel completely embarrassed. But I have no idea about what I have or have not been doing." She left after thanking him and agreeing to let him know if she had further questions. She had a zillion. The first one: Where was the closest place she could buy some aspirin?

How was Marianne going to tell her parents that she wanted to have control of her own financial information? Well, she had control in the office and in her personal life, and now she wanted to understand more about what, how, and why she should do things financially. First she was going to find out if her bank had a tax-free money market fund and what the current rate was. If they did, maybe she would switch into that fund. She'd have to calculate what she was keeping after taxes in the regular money market fund and compare it to the rate of the tax-free fund. That would help her make that decision. And the next time she asked Richard a question and he just winked at her, she was going to tell him off.

In the end Marianne did switch to a tax-free money market fund, but she never went back to Richard. The next year when she was getting ready to do her taxes she told her father that she had decided to go to someone else. That was fine with him. It was just that simple. He hadn't meant to be autocratic; he had simply been worried. Even though Marianne had been successful in her own business, she hadn't appeared to be interested in finances. He could tell now that her money mattered to her, and he respected that. Now that he knew that she wanted to understand her own finances, he had no issue with whom she went to for advice. In fact, he was very proud of her.

It was a little scary at first, but she got better and better at asking what she used to refer to as "stupid questions." As a matter of fact, the stupider the question seemed, the more she knew she had better ask it.

What was most interesting about all this was that Marianne was getting good at understanding what was being explained to her. You see, she had just never asked before. She had been too concerned about not looking smart or not being able to understand.

"The friends," as they called themselves, met routinely for dinner. They were considering taking classes in investing.

"Let's go together so we can study together," Hope suggested.

"Okay, if it's on a Tuesday," said Marianne.

They all enrolled at the New School. Feeling like kids again, they marched themselves to class for one entire semester to learn more about investing.

They started learning about **fixed income investments. Bonds** are called fixed income investments because they pay a predetermined amount of interest at specific periods of time on a regular schedule. They are like IOUs. You lend your money to the government, a city, state, or municipality, or to a corporation and they agree to pay you (the creditor) back interest at predetermined time intervals and then pay back the principal at a preset time too. On the other hand, if the value of the company goes up, you don't get to participate. That's for the stockholders.

They took classes on investing in the **stock** market. When you invest in stock you become a shareholder in the company. If the company does well, you do well; if the company doesn't profit, neither do you. You might receive dividends, and that is considered income each year. Those dividends are paid out to the investor from the profits of the company.

They were surprised to find out that about 20 percent of the population of the United States owns stock.

The class the friends liked best taught about diversification. It actually fits into my favorite rule about investing too. As my Bubbie used to say, *"It's not the best thing to put all your eggs in one basket."* Well, maybe she didn't make up the saying, but she sure did use it often.

The women went to class eager to learn which would be the best investment for them. What they learned was very interesting. Bubbie was right!

Diversification is the best protection in dealing with risk. Portfolios that are diversified have investments in many areas. They have **liquid investments** that are easily available. These are also known as **cash equivalents.** They include **money market funds, certificates of deposit,** and **Treasury bills.**

A good portfolio will have bonds as well as stocks, and depending on economic changes or an imbalance in the growth of the portfolio, some switches may be made to balance things out over time.

The reason for this diversification or mixed basket is that different investments tend to do well at different times. This reduces the overall **volatility** of assets. *There is no one best investment.*

Marianne loved the classes and the opportunity to learn and ask questions about financial planning. So had her friends. They loved sharing this back-to-school adventure and being kids again with each other. They got to ask questions (including all the stupid ones), shared their stories, and understood what they hadn't a short time before.

Next term they are taking classes in understanding the basics of retirement planning.

Can You Figure Out the Plot?

You know how one conversation leads you into another, and then before you know it you're on an entirely different topic? That's just what happened with Frederica.

August 15 was the deadline to make a Keogh contribution for Frederica, who had previously filed with the Internal Revenue Service requesting an extension to pay her income taxes and file her tax return. Normally people pay their taxes and fund their retirement plans by April 15, but Frederica needed more time to get her information together, so her accountant requested an extension. It was two days before the deadline, so she called me to see if she could drop by to visit, hand in the check for deposit to her account, maybe talk for a few minutes, and then visit Century 21, a very well known discount department store conveniently across the street from my office. She probably would have sent the check in overnight or by messenger if it weren't for the lure of that great discount store.

We had met a couple of years earlier when I spoke to a group of professional women about how to begin to be comfortable about planning for the rest of their lives. These were pretty smart women in their forties, all respected in their field, who had never taken the time to look at their lives in a preplanned way. That's not to say they didn't have most of what they needed. It was more that they didn't know *what* they had, and as a result didn't know what, if anything, needed to be changed or even considered. What's new! So I got together with them to outline the kinds of things that they might want to look at and consider. We only had an hour together, but that was enough time to go over some of the basics. We reviewed the concepts of **investment planning** and the fact that choosing the right investments has to do with an individual's risk tolerance and personal financial circumstances, as well as general market conditions. **Insurance planning, or risk management**, is an important part of financial planning and includes life insurance, disability insurance, and long-term care. **Retirement planning** is critical, based on the fact that most people will still need 70 to 80 percent of their salaries adjusted for inflation when they retire. **Estate planning** handles the issues of what is left, how, and to whom, when you die.

Frederica decided to visit me with her husband Bruce. I like to work with people face-to-face. I would hardly expect a doctor to conduct an office visit with me over the phone. Trust is a big part of making things happen, and being with each other helps build relationships. Sort of like show-and-tell. Once you have planned together and set up a strategy, you can work on things that come up later over the phone if necessary, but it's always better to be with each other in the beginning.

We had worked together for a while now and done whatever planning was required for the short term. I hadn't seen Frederica in months, so it was nice that she was coming for a visit.

"I've gotta tell you a story," she said. "We all had a laugh talking about you the other day at the meeting of our women's group. Remember when you spoke and said that it would be an important thing in our lives if we could take our ability to earn money more seriously? That we should all get disability insurance just in case of an emergency to protect ourselves against lost income? Remember how we debated about the cost and whether we could afford it or not? And you said you'd like us to think about if we could afford to take the risk not to do it. You made a good point: We insure our cars hoping that we will never get into an accident and never think twice about whether that is a good idea; in fact, we hope that the premiums get wasted. If you don't have an accident you don't get your money back, and that's just fine. Well, we did it—we are all insured now. We were laughing with each other and saying that Eileen would be so proud if she knew that we had all done what we said we would. I think we all feel a lot safer now. Anyway, I do."

It was important for these women to have disability insurance. Workers between the ages of 35 and 65 are six times more likely to be disabled than to die! Disability insurance is bought to replace income and support a family in the event of disaster when you can't work. The income of these ladies was important to their families' well-being.

I did feel proud—I had just gotten a gift. It's nice to be appreciated and told when things work well.

"Anyway," Frederica continued, "recently a couple of people close to us have gotten really sick, and that began to bring everything home. We realized that we don't have cemetery plots. We hadn't considered dying until this point and now here we are confronted with the mortality of our friends and I guess ourselves. So we asked ourselves, How would Eileen handle this? Someone in the group suggested that you'd probably say, 'Do it whatever way you can, but do it.' So, we've all made a date to go cemetery-plot shopping, a little something like a day at Loehmann's, just not exactly. It would be nice if we could all be together in the same cemetery with our plots near each other."

After she left I was thinking about my own choices. The offices in the big cemeteries in New York remind me of shopping in a supermarket. You see large signs hanging, as if at the deli counter, that say:

PERPETUAL CARE $2,000
YEWS $445
BLUE SPRUCE $500

When you go up to the counter to find out where a funeral is going to be held or where the gravestone of a loved one is, they need to look in the computer: "Aisle 9 Plot 11. Make a left at Mount Sinai Avenue, a right on Elm Street, a left near the Elk Society plot and then halfway in you should find it." Sounds something like "aisle five past the toiletries and a left at the paper goods." This just does not work for me.

What would work for me? What would I like done with my remains after I die? After they give away all my usable parts I'm going to be cremated. My mother says that it doesn't leave anybody a place to visit where they can mourn me, but I just don't see it that way. I rarely go to the cemetery to visit grave sites. My friends and family live in my heart. This book, for instance, and the stories I tell are their perpetual memorials. So I've decided not to be in a cemetery.

On a recent visit to Canada to spend time with my kids, we started to talk about insurance and wills. Now that they have children themselves, they are concerned about protecting their family. And the conversation got around to what I would like them to do with me when I die. It was nice of them to ask. So I told them. First, I'd like to be cremated. Then I'd like the ashes to be divided in three parts—three unequal parts: 50 percent, 25 percent, 25 percent. I figured that maybe it would be hard on my boys if they had no place to go to visit me, even though they say now, as I have always said, that they probably will never want to go there. In the end they will mourn any way they want, but I've given them some specific instructions that would please me as well, just in case. So I think I may have worked out a fabulous solution.

The first 50 percent I'd like scattered in a park. I don't care which one. Just put me in a place that's big and bright, where people play, where children run and trees grow. Cemeteries are great if they are tiny, in the back of a church or synagogue in some small town, but the big ones leave me feeling lonely. I'd rather be part of land where lots of people are around. For the balance, I'd like each of the boys and their families to take one of the other two remaining packs and put me in a lead can. Then I'd like them to bury me in their front lawns . . . right near a statue of a Madonna, a rosebush, and a floodlight. That way they won't have to go far to visit me and they can dig me out and take me whenever they move, wherever they go, and my grandchildren can point me out to their friends.

Doesn't this sound just like a typical financial adviser: allocation and diversification.

You think I'm kidding, right? Maybe. But I have left instructions. Have you?

At Every Turn

Credit, debt, inflation, taxes, retirement, savings, investments, benefits . . . some grown-up words.

When you were a child, and for many of us way into adolescence and early adulthood, what meaning did these words carry? None. These were the words of responsibility and age. Well, come on in and sit right down. You have arrived.

One hundred years ago the average life expectancy was 50. So if your grandparents never seemed to be worried about outliving their money, that was probably because they weren't planning on outliving their money! No need to have to plan for old age then. Maybe they retired if they could afford to, and they lived a few years more and then they died. Today we can expect to live way into our eighties and many can expect to hit 100. That alone can cause one to sit up and think about life differently. For sure, it makes even the 20-year-olds start to focus on the what-ifs of life.

Even though no one fits exactly into nice little niches, there are some things that appear to be truer than not about money stages. We plan for retirement and assume that we will need less then—maybe. What would it take to produce even 70 percent of what we think we will need for retirement assuming that pensions and Social Security will make up the difference?

Your Twenties:

Maybe in your early twenties you are still in school or working at your first job. Could be that you are sharing your home with your parents or one, two, or more roommates. Or perhaps, let's try this scenario: You are married, maybe you have a child. In any case, unless you have been the recipient of a trust fund or are a wunderkind on Wall Street, you probably have *cash flow problems.* There just hasn't been much preparation time to learn about money management. Even if you were trained within the household, it was based on your parents' experiences and beliefs, and life after all has been changing. You know how excited you were when you filled out your credit card application in your very own name and the first credit card showed up in the mailbox. No need to let all that extra cash go to waste, right? I mean if they gave you the card, they must have expected you to use it. Just remember, those minimum monthly bills that start showing up in your mailbox can be killers. You may be paying off college debts and struggling to meet living expenses. But you're young and just getting started.

You think, No need to worry about health benefits. I'm young and healthy, and retirement, that's way in the future. But *if you did put away 10 percent of your income from your early twenties until age 65 you would have saved enough to replace about 70 percent of your income and would have most of what you need for retirement.*

Your Thirties:

No real planning yet. If you're not married, you want to go places, see things, not just work and hibernate. Maybe you're in graduate school. Did you just get an apartment of your own? If you are married, you are both working hard to pay all the bills, try to have a decent place to live, and take care of the kids if there are any. Child care costs are sometimes one-half or more of the second parent's income—and that's for just one child. Maybe you are thinking about your child's college tuition. Perhaps there's thought of life insurance. There may be little left of your paycheck and you have become aware of the ugly sisters: inflation and taxation. These girls eat away at your income and reduce your buying power.

Historically, the rate of **inflation** in the United States has been around 4 percent. Some years it has been much higher and other years the rate has been close to zero. But basically, on average your dollar buys 4 percent less every year than it did the year before. You have to increase your paycheck by that amount just to break even. Compare costs in 1963, the year that John F. Kennedy was assassinated, with the costs of 1995:

	1963	1995
cost of a luxury car	$3,800	$36,000
movie ticket	$1.00	$7.50
cup of coffee	$.10	$.75
gallon of gas	$.30	$1.40
U.S. postage stamp	$.05	$.32

At these rates, in thirty years, the time of retirement that most 30-year-olds plan on, a cup of coffee will cost $5.52 and a movie at a local theater will cost $55 or so. That can prove to be a hell of a night out. If the business where you are working is offering a retirement plan, the probability is that you are not yet participating fully, if at all. *If you start putting 15 percent of your earnings away for investment for use at retirement, you will have saved enough to replace approximately 70 percent of your income at retirement.*

Your Forties:

Big bills of many shapes and sizes showing up? College costs, mortgage costs, building a business, starting over, new babies, older parents? Forty is one of those consciousness-raising ages. Weren't you supposed to have been somewhere financially by now? How could you have been?

Are you still single and beginning to reflect on what you will need to get where you want to go? There may not be that partner you were planning on sharing things with.

You may be aware that 50 percent of the time that you had to prepare for retirement is just about used up. Are your parents getting older? Are new concepts like elder care and long-term care cropping up in conversations? Are your dental bills getting larger? Is your health care policy a concern? Are you not only talking about having more roughage in your diet over lunch but about creating living wills and health care proxies?

If you are in your forties and have a new baby, she will be in college at the same time that you are close to retirement. The double whammy!

In your forties and have a baby or two *and* a parent that you may need to help? Maybe this is your second family, with the same or maybe a new partner. Feeling a little like the filling of a sandwich?

Remember that all the money that you put in your children's names, planning to use for their college tuition, will become theirs at the age of majority. They don't have to go to school or be nice or visit you often; they just need to be of majority.

You may even be thinking that now you really need to get involved with creating a formal plan. Seems to be time to create some order.

If you start saving at 40 and continue through age 65, you will have to save 21 percent of your current income to replace 70 percent of your income at retirement.

Your Fifties:

For some of you, life has taken an upturn. You are making more money than ever before. The kids are in good shape and you have more than enough to cover the bills. You have been good at following your plan, if not perfect, and you have savings and investments and have prepared for the future. If you are single, you are handling all the same issues and you are enjoying life. Or maybe you are not. For many of us, 50 shows up very fast! Faster than we planned. Maybe for some of us, nothing is in place. You have witnessed early retirement, or perhaps illness, and the thought of how you will live out the next thirty years of your life can make you queasy. We are all good at filing these concerns in the back of our minds.

By now many of you will have experienced the death of parents. Did you have to deal with attorneys and wills and courts? If you have children, you have dealt with college applications, requests for student aid. Hang in there: you will pay off the mortgage someday, your children will grow up and reduce some of your financial pressure. Perhaps you may inherit some money from someone kind!

If you've waited until age 50 to start to invest and plan for retirement then you will need to save 48 percent of your income to replace 70 percent income at age 65.

Your Sixties:

So here you are . . . how did time go so fast? It seems that we just started making plans, new beginnings, life changes. You may have grandchildren; perhaps you're retired or getting ready to retire; you may have lost a spouse or a life partner. Now your focus is on the next thirty years: making sure that your investments and pension will work for you. Have you met with an attorney yet to handle concerns about *your* estate? Whom have you identified to make decisions should you be unable to? Or, are you not even thinking about retirement? Plenty of vital people continue to work well into their eighties if they can, and if they are not restricted by their employers. With that in mind, with your finances somewhat settled, I hope that you have given yourself permission to enjoy every day. Some of you may have never worked, or were already retired. Your parents may still be alive and you are retired at the same time they are. You will find that along with the new group you have joined, the "Silvers," there are lots of benefits being offered to senior citizens. Senior citizens have a lot of power in this country and are growing stronger in voice every day.

We are no longer children, and money matters all the time, at every turn. It matters to each of us in different ways, but always for the life lessons that we have been taught through it. Its power is with us always.

Get Over It,
Get On with It,
and Get a Sense of Humor

You want to know the best cure for moving on after you've messed things up? Yes, even if you've been bad with money, even if you've done things that you find yourself disgusted with, there is something you can do to start putting the pieces together. You can implement this advice immediately while you are in the process of righting your wrongs, and it won't cost you anything. That's right, a no-cost opportunity! *Get over it, get on with it, and get a sense of humor.* Those are the first three rules of dealing with money problems.

I don't mean to trivialize your feelings or difficult experiences, but they are in the past. Even your great, powerful, outstanding moments are history. Use these times to learn and grow, and promise yourself not to repeat whatever miserable and awful mistakes you have made. This is a new beginning!

Do you get on your own case and can't get off it? Do you really think that serves any purpose? You keep telling your stories to other people, who probably have stories that are just as good or better. They are probably nodding and listening out of respect, but frankly, for the most part they don't care. It isn't their money. They realize that you are *not* looking for advice, just a good ear, and so they offer that. Hey, they have their own problems and may soon want your ear. Sometimes they'll even be glad it's not them who has the problem and will be happy to sit and nod while you go over and over what happened, what you should have done, and how stupid you were. But after a while it just gets boring. You may find that if you listen to yourself carefully you are getting bored too. Enough already!

Yes, women are the storytellers. We create stories and share them. We edit and embellish them, pass them along and teach with them. But we can also use these fine stories as a way of not moving on. It's comfortable. We like to live in the world of the in-betweens, not black or white. Our stories are usually filled with shades of gray and often never end. Packed with emotion, they can make *Gone With the Wind* sound like a comic strip. We say, "Let me explain," or "There was a reason." We tell version after version of the same story, with new twists—we hold on, we just can't let go. Sometimes we just can't get off that dime. We are afraid of moving on, and that's what we need to do most. *If we want our money matters to be different than they have been up until now, then we need to get on with handling things.* Ultimately, action—getting on with it—is what makes things happen. It's our opportunity to have things be different.

Yes, a new plan of action is called for. This will feel strange, because you are calling on yourself to stretch new muscles and think new thoughts. So be kind to yourself—not overindulgent, but please do be kind! Don't beat yourself up. Think of the times when you have done a new form of physical labor and how sore you became. The advice always is to take a day of rest, relax, and start again. It's the same here. Take a hard look at the situation and see what lessons you've learned. Then use them. You want to know what I mean by that? Well, it's like this: Most of us have done or maybe failed to do things that we now sit back and judge. Either we waited too long to jump on an opportunity and lost it, or we jumped too soon and now feel that we should have been more diligent or smarter. We didn't ask enough questions, or we trusted someone else more than we trusted our own instincts. We did what we thought was expected of us because we wanted to look good or make people like us. Sometimes we didn't speak out on our behalf because we didn't want to look selfish or upset someone. We didn't want to be known as insensitive or power hungry. We didn't take action because we were nervous, or we jumped too quickly without doing the needed research because we just wanted to get done with it or look smart. Most of the time, we did what we did because we thought it was the best decision to make at the time, but *regardless of how things have turned out in the past, it is over and done now and it can teach us if we are open to the lessons.*

Years ago, after my friend Ken (you remember Ken) and I started investing in real estate in Virginia, we were doing extraordinarily well. God yes! Everyone was doing well in real estate in the late eighties. Two other men wanted to be our partners and help get more financing than we could have possibly dreamed of. Hey, no problem. The bigger the better.

We started to accumulate properties like the pieces on a Monopoly board. I felt great. What should I be worried about? I was in business with three men who had extensive experience in real estate and the construction industry; two of them were attorneys. How much better could it get? Sure, I was signing my name on all the mortgages, but so were they, and they were worth lots more than I was. They had much more at risk. Or did they?

You see, it came to pass that the real estate market went to hell sometime around 1990, and my partners had lost much of their net worth because most of their investments had been in real estate. Real estate is a funny kind of investment because it's highly **leveraged.** You put down a payment of 10 percent and borrow the other 90 percent from the bank. If all goes well, as we always expect it to when we make investments, we can make money, very good money. But if the value of property goes down, it is possible to lose money, more than the original down payment. Because of the leverage used in financing mortgages, as Donald Trump can tell you, real estate is a tricky game. If you have rental property and the rent you expect to get stops coming in or drops because of a bad economic cycle, you still need to make your mortgage payments.

By now, two of my strong, no-problem partners were unemployed and on the verge of bankruptcy, and one had to go back into law practice after years of running a construction company. The last building we had built wasn't carrying itself by a long shot, and the mortgage needed to be paid. Lo and behold, I was the only one of the bunch holding down a job. This was not good news! Suffice it to say I was not happy. How could I have been so foolish as to get myself into this position? After all, hadn't I known better, wasn't I in the money business? But here I was, and now what?

First things first. I called upon my innermost being to find the humor in all this. And it *was* funny. Here I was the girl, the low "man" on the totem pole, ending up the most vulnerable and valuable with the bank, because after all was said and done my income was the only thing the bank could bet on. That was my lesson. When I got into all of this I should have asked myself how I would feel if no one else could make the payments. Perhaps I should have realized my partners had paper wealth but not real dollars in the bank to protect us if something went wrong. Better save that for next time!

Now I realized that I had better do something different from what I had done in the past. The men had made all the decisions about this project before, because they were the experts. What should I do? I needed to be in charge of the group instead of waiting for the guys to make the decisions. They were struggling to survive; this project that we were doing together was not the only ongoing project for them, but it was for me. I had better get with the program. It worked. Once we put our heads together, we started to look at all the options that were available to us. My partners agreed that we would speak to the bank, put the building in trouble up for sale, and pay for the legal fees. That was painful but not deadly. At least there were choices being made, and actions being taken. Things were starting to look hopeful again. I was starting to breathe. And I am happy to report that all the other buildings are rented and prospering.

Remember that, after all, we have also made successful decisions too. We have taken on new life experiences related to money and finance and have been proved right. We have begun careers, changed them, married, lived alone or with significant others, been single parents, put ourselves or our children through school. We have been extraordinary employees and bosses. We've bought homes and cars and started savings and retirement plans. And yet we rarely give ourselves credit for these accomplishments. What we did, we just did. We think, Oh well, that's what I was supposed to do. But what we did unsuccessfully we do blame ourselves for and say we did wrong. We hunker down and stop ourselves from moving on. If a friend told you her story, you'd probably appreciate the circumstances, support her in understanding what happened, and suggest she stop being so hard on herself. But that's because you're talking to her and not to yourself. Women usually are kinder and more understanding of someone else. Most men have learned how to live by doing this process differently.

They realize that they may make mistakes, that in fact most people who take risks do make mistakes, that it's just part of the learning curve. Women get stuck here. It's time to get on with it.

Maybe the reason why we have such a hard time moving on is that we don't understand what has stopped us in the first place. Sometimes our money issues are not that easily understood. We tend to fix on being smarter, shrewder, and sharper. Yes, those things are important, but not as important as understanding the issues we each have about entitlement, responsibility, security, risk, and how we make our choices. They are struggles about power—of how and where we can and should be powerful. Having too much debt, or failing to read our financial statements, or not planning for the future, or placing ourselves last on the list of people with needs to be handled—that is how these issues often reveal themselves. If we understood the underlying struggles, we would not be such harsh self-critics. We make our financial decisions based on a lot more than our bank balances or cash flow. We make most of our decisions based on how we *feel* about things, and how we feel is a complicated matter.

We often prefer not to deal in hard facts. We don't like to say, "I lost money in the stock market," or "I want my money back" to someone we've lent it to, or "I want a raise and this is what I'm worth." We sometimes don't like to read bank statements, or brokerage statements. Sometimes we act as if they are report cards from school and we don't think we'll like what we will see. "Better not to think about it. After all," we say, "if I don't balance my account or focus on how much I owe, it will be better for my nerves. I can't deal with everything. I would ask my cousin Joe for the money he owes me, but it could cause a problem in the family and my mother would just drive me crazy. I don't want to be driven crazy on top of everything that's going on in my life." Yes, of course; but if you asked Joe for the money, you might have less debt, which in turn would lower the stress you are currently experiencing—but that's another story. We will get around to it someday, and that thought pacifies us for a while.

Britta never balanced her checkbook. She just hated doing it because she just could never get the numbers to work out right. It made her feel incompetent and anxious. Her solution was to know "around" how much she had, always leaving a couple of hundred dollars extra in the account that she never added in. Then one day, after a check bounced because of poor addition, she decided to master the beast. This just couldn't go on anymore; she was tired of running away. Oh, sweet surrender. After she did her calculating and figuring, she determined that when all was said and done there was $35 less than she had "guesstimated." A pretty embarrassing math mistake. Well, she had known that she was cutting it close, but she had been too busy to go to the ATM machine and move money from her savings account to her checking account. She hated trying to guess how much money she had, but her plan of keeping a slush fund just in case she guessed wrong hadn't worked.

What she decided to do was call the bank each Friday and find out exactly what her balance was and what checks had cleared. That way she would always be on top of things. Now the customer service rep knows her voice and they have this great working relationship. She doesn't have to deal with that fat envelope that shows up in her mailbox once a month that holds her statements. She no longer has to give up an evening of her time to try to balance the account. Now she has a system that is manageable. Better yet, she is handling her money instead of being handled by it. Great idea? Of course that was a great idea; all it took was a little creativity and the willingness to move on.

Remember, even the decision to do nothing is a decision. And you are responsible for making *that* decision. So what if you avoid looking at your bill from the credit card company? You still owe the money. You still have the same bank balance, be the envelope opened or not. Not asking for what you think you deserve doesn't give you more sleep at night, it probably gives you less. And if you could have a sense of humor about these matters, you would probably be able to laugh a little more and suffer a little less. Usually after you start to move on—to get on with it—life starts to feel a whole lot better. You have the opportunity to retell your story with a different perspective and create a different ending.

Anyway, whatever you have done in the past, *you* can create a new way of living in the future. *You* can change your relationship to money and *you will* if you want to, if you allow yourself the opportunity to move things one step at a time. A clear look at what is going on with you and your relationship to money will free you up, give you room to breathe, lighten your load so that you can move on.

And yes, get a sense of humor, especially if you've let yours lapse along the way. It is a major component of life. It costs nothing and it is contagious.

Now, stand back and watch yourself for a week. How do you handle your money stuff? Be a witness. Don't judge, just watch. Have some compassion for the person you are observing—she's really a good woman. What have you learned about yourself? Not bad?

Are you willing to move on? You need permission? OKAY, YOU'VE GOT IT!

Facts We Learned:

CHOICES

Tax deferred means postponing the payment of taxes: retirement plans, annuities.

Tax free means no current or future tax is paid: municipal bonds.

In order to protect your income in the event of illness, the purchase of disability insurance should be considered.

Profit-sharing plans and money purchase plans can be used as retirement plans for investors who have businesses. The maximum annual contribution for one plan is $22,500. The maximum for both plans is $30,000.

Fixed income investments are fixed as to rate of return.

Common stock holders are owners of the corporation.

Lessons We Learned:

CHOICES

We are always making choices.

Even the choice of not choosing is a choice.

We can change what we want, how we want to do it, and if we want to, at any time.

It is always better to make an informed choice.

It is our perception of entitlement, responsibility, security, and risk that directly affects the way we choose.

SOME BOOKS
YOU MAY WANT TO READ

Here's a list of some books that I have recommended to clients that are user friendly and sensitive to the fact that not everyone interested in money and finance has an MBA or is getting one. They do not have to be read from cover to cover. They can be used as resource, from time to time, when a question arises. Some of them have great pictures and diagrams.

The Beardstown Ladies Investment Club with Leslie Whitaker. *The Beardstown Ladies Commonsense Guide to Investments.* Boston: Little Brown, 1994.

CarolAnn Brown. *100 Questions Every Working American Must Ask.* Michigan: Dearborn Financial Publishing, 1996.

Kenneth M. Morris and Alan M. Siegel. *The Wall Street Journal Guide to Planning Your Financial Future: The Easy-to-Read Guide to Planning for Retirement.* New York: Lightbulb Press and Dow Jones and Company, 1995.

Kenneth M. Morris, Scott R. Schmedel, Alan M. Siegel. *The Wall Street Journal Guide to Understanding Your Taxes.* New York: Lightbulb Press and Dow Jones and Company, 1995.

Kenneth M. Morris and Alan M. Siegel. *The Wall Street Journal Guide to Understanding Money and Investing.* New York: Lightbulb Press and Dow Jones and Company, 1995.

Kenneth M. Morris and Alan M. Siegel. *The Wall Street Journal Guide to Understanding Personal Finance.* New York: Lightbulb Press and Dow Jones and Company, 1995.

Eric Tyson. *Personal Finance for Dummies.* IDG Books Worldwide, 1994.

DATE DUE			